Penguin Handbooks
Food as Presents

Patricia Holden White grew up on a farm in rural America. She
worked as an editor at a New York publishing house before
moving to England at the end of the sixties. Now working in
London as a literary agent, she lives with a lurcher called Quince
and a cat called Bliss. *Food as Presents* is her fourth cookery
book.

Food as Presents

Patricia Holden White
With drawings by M. J. Mott

Penguin Books

Penguin Books Ltd, Harmondsworth, Middlesex, England
Penguin Books, 625 Madison Avenue, New York, New York 10022, U.S.A.
Penguin Books Australia Ltd, Ringwood, Victoria, Australia
Penguin Books Canada Ltd, 2801 John Street, Markham, Ontario, Canada L3R 1B4
Penguin Books (N.Z.) Ltd, 182–190 Wairau Road, Auckland 10, New Zealand

First published by Faber and Faber 1975
Revised and expanded edition published in Penguin Books 1982

Copyright © Patricia Holden White, 1975, 1982

Made and printed in Great Britain by
Richard Clay (The Chaucer Press) Ltd, Bungay, Suffolk
Set in Monophoto Plantin

For
Loved Ones
Everywhere

Contents

Contents

Potted foods 65

Savoury cocktail nibbles 81

Sweet sauces 87

Contents

Sweetmeats 93

Baked goods 105

Alcoholic drinks and preserves   133

Index   142

Metric
conversion tables

For the purpose of conversion to metric measure,
I have used the following equivalents:

1 oz = 25 g
1 lb = 400 g
2½ lb = 1 kg
½ pt = ¼ litre = 250 millitres
1 pt = ½ litre = 500 millitres
2 pts = 1 litre = 1000 millitres

Note: all temperatures given in the recipes are in degrees
Fahrenheit.

°Fahrenheit	Gas Mark	°Centigrade
225	¼	110
250	½	130
275	1	140
300	2	150
325	3	170
350	4	180
375	5	190
400	6	200
425	7	220
450	8	230
475	9	240

Introduction

At a time when almost every food under the sun is available in the shops, if only one has the money and time, how satisfactory it is to give presents from one's own kitchen. Such presents express beyond the measure of money the caring of the giver. The variety of possible produce is endless, without having to worry about the gift being the wrong size or colour.

I started giving food as presents quite accidentally. Although my childhood was spent on a farm in the country, when I grew up I found myself living in city apartments, with lamentably small kitchens and economic, to say the least, storage space. Envy exuded from every pore when I visited country friends who made jams, jellies and wonderful chutneys, whose shelves were filled with admirable rows of shining jars neatly labelled. Preserving at home was for me a very country thing which clearly had to be done in quantity. The summers of my childhood were punctuated by the production of wild strawberry jam and blueberry marmalade in batches to last the year, with enormous preserving pans constantly bubbling. A sure sign that I was growing up was being allowed to stir the hot jam. Somehow preserving and childhood, and nostalgia for the two together, drifted into memory as I became a city dweller. Despite having written three cookbooks and thinking of myself as a competent cook, preserving pans, jelly bags and neatly labelled jars seemed a long way off. I did occasionally make a pâté or a batch of the 'richest brownies known to man' as a present, but the concept of giving food as presents had not yet become a reality for me.

Then my life turned around. I gave up New York for London, a well-paid job for a literary agent's commission, and became, hard to believe, the possessor of an even smaller kitchen. By my first Christmas in England, it became evident that I would have to do something creative in the present line. So many people had been kind in helping me to find my feet in a new life that I wanted to say 'thank you' in a personal way. I could not afford to do so with lavish presents but wanted to give something personal that would give pleasure without the embarrassment of bought presents. That Christmas saw me buying my first preserving pan – wondering what else I could cook in it – and the production of a Herculean batch of lemon curd. The sight of my first row of shining jars and neatly written labels gave me so much pleasure that I very nearly didn't give them away! It was the beginning.

From lemon curd, I began to make things that I missed from home that were impossible, or nearly so, to find in England, or were at such a premium that they were far beyond my limited budget. Corn and pepper relish, watermelon pickle, real chilli sauce and bread and butter pickles were among my first produce. These I made for my own consumption, and found that guests hung about the kitchen staring pointedly at rows of things I had made. Finally, the penny dropped and my present-giving problems were solved forever. There isn't an occasion I can think of for which an attractively packaged food present isn't appropriate. I've even given collections of jams, vinegars, fruits in brandy, etc., done up prettily in hampers as wedding presents.

I now make all the marmalade, jam, vinegars and pickles consumed in my house, as well as baked goods, simply because I think, rightly or wrongly, that I make them better (and certainly more cheaply) than I can buy them. This does take planning ahead, but one soon develops a sense of how much is likely to be eaten in a period of time, on top of which I reckon on an approximate amount to be used as presents throughout the year. This isn't a very exact computation, and you may find yourself running out of one thing and having too much of another, but a mental note for next year will rectify things. If you develop a passion for making preserves, as happened to me, things can get out of hand and you may find yourself with marmalade stored under the bed, for want of any other available place to put it. I would suggest starting off production in a limited way, making things in small batches, rather than in one large batch, particularly if you are using a recipe for the first time. Not only will you be able to control the quantity of what you produce, but if disaster ensues (jams not jelling, vinegar clouding, etc.), and alas, we all have culinary disasters at some point, it will simply be on a smaller scale.

Food as presents falls into two categories – food to be made in season to be enjoyed throughout the year (jams, pickles, preserved fruit, etc.) and food to be made near the time of giving and consumption (pâtés, baked goods, candies etc.). Happily the freezer has extended the life of the second category, and now many once perishable foods can be made when one has the time and inclination, to be brought out of the freezer later on to give.

Lest this book drone on for many volumes, I have not included every jam, jelly, pickle, biscuit, cake, candy, bread and pâté recipe known to man. There are so many marvellous basic cookbooks whose pages are filled with variations of the more obvious presents from your kitchen. I hope what I have done is to set you thinking about giving food as presents and its practicability for everyone. Included with the recipes are ideas about keeping your produce at the peak of flavour and colour, and advice on packaging and mailing.

General notes
on labelling, storing
and posting

Labelling

Jars or bottles containing preserves, vinegars or sauces should always be clearly labelled as to contents and date of making, as should containers of potted meat, seafood or cheese. And any food intended for freezing should be labelled in this way. Things do not last in pristine shape indefinitely in the freezer and the date on the label will call attention to the weeks slipping by. It is also a good idea to add the date by which the food would best be eaten.

Typewritten labels are easiest to read. If you are handwriting labels, the writing should be easily legible and in ballpoint pen (a splash of water on writing in ink will obscure the label). You can buy sheets of self-adhesive labels, with or without coloured borders, and many stationery or speciality printers now print labels that say 'From the kitchen of' or the like. Don't put labels on with sellotape as it yellows and peels. Self-adhesive labels are always best for food that is to be frozen.

Storing

All food not kept in the refrigerator or freezer is best kept in cool places with a good circulation of air, and preserves and vinegars are best kept in the dark as well. A hot kitchen cupboard is likely to produce jars of quickly moulding, cloudy jam. You would be far better off storing jars and bottles in a dry cupboard in the garage or basement (if it's cool) or in a sheltered spot on a balcony or fire escape. Nothing brings home the importance of proper storage more than making a splendid lot of jam in summer, ready for Christmas giving, to find on 23 December that you have a cupboard full of mouldy jam rapidly turning to sugar.

It isn't always easy to find a dark, cool, dry spot, particularly in centrally heated conditions, but a little ingenuity and thought should yield the answer. I have a friend who has given up growing flowers in window boxes – they die of pollution, she says – and uses the window boxes to store jam jars in, wrapped in polythene bags from the drycleaners to beat the dampness problem and covered with an old plastic tablecloth to keep out the light. She also introduced me to the idea of keeping jars and bottles under the bed when all other space is used up. It is a little startling when making the bed, but effective (provided, of course, that your bedroom is fairly cool!)

Posting

Put whatever (preferably unbreakable and *not* glass) container you are using into a cardboard box about twice the size of the container and surround it with tightly wadded up newspaper, wood or paper shavings, or any clean used paper, so there is no movement whatever in the box. If the box has a lid, use it; otherwise fold over the 4 free parts that form the top and seal with sellotape before over-wrapping the parcel with brown paper and securing well with string. The label should be typed or written in ballpoint pen and should carry your return address. Mark the parcel in bold letters 'FOOD – FRAGILE', and off to the Post Office. I don't know why I assume that because I care about getting food presents to friends in pristine condition the Post Office will too, but so far I've been successful.

Preserves

Preserving

Remember when making preserves that *no homemade preserve lasts forever in a pristine state*. Commercially made preserves do last better because they are filled with additives designed to keep them in a highly colourful, unchanging state – no matter whether they taste of nothing and are plastic in texture! Obviously there are many creditable mass-produced preserves, but for variety and freshness you can't beat homemade.

You can help the durability of the preserves you make considerably by:

1 choosing fruit wisely if you are making jelly or jam (see p. 26);
2 being scrupulous about using hot sterilized jars (see below);
3 filling jars to the brim, or to within ⅛ inch of the top if making jelly or jam or chutney (leaving just enough space for a waxed disc or coating of paraffin wax). This is important because it eliminates air space in the jar in which yeasts can develop, leading to fermentation or mould;
4 using waxed discs or paraffin wax on top of jam, jelly or chutney (see p. 29) and sealing all jars well so that they are absolutely airtight;
5 never sealing jars when contents are lukewarm. This applies mainly to jams, jellies and chutneys;
6 storing filled jars in cool, dark places with a good circulation of air (see general notes on storing, p. 16).

Sterilizing jars: wash jars in soap and water, rinse them out and turn upside down to drain. Put jars in a roasting pan with an inch of water in the bottom and put in a 300° (mark 2) oven for about 15 minutes, until the water is almost bubbling, the jars too hot to touch and the insides competely dry.

Jars

For *jams and jellies* any uncracked jar is fair game. If it has a screw-on lid so much the better. If it does have a screw-on lid, be sure to remove any cardboard liner that it contains before using. To establish the airtightness of a lid, fill the jar with water, screw on the lid tightly, dry the outside of the jar and leave it on your draining board upside down. If moisture escapes you would be best advised not to use the lid but to use a plastic wrap cover secured with an elastic band. You want your jam jar as airtight as possible.

Jars with plastic screw tops, like instant coffee jars, are best used for chutneys. Plastic tops aren't a hundred per cent airtight and can encourage mouldy jam; but are fine for vinegar-based preserves. Baby food jars are a good choice if you want to give a selection of jams to one person. You will find the promise of a sample of what you are making will keep your friends supplying you with every jar they possess. Jars can be used over and over again, provided they don't get cracked. Lids do get loose, however, so be careful to check for dents and cracks that may let air into the jar. Also be sure to watch for rust and deterioration on the inside of lids that are used over and over. Discard these lids at the first sign. Don't use any lids other than screw-on ones.

If the price has been stamped on the top of a lid, a quick scrub with scouring powder should take it off, and a coat of enamel obliterates the lettering on the top of some lids. Repainting lids helps to entertain children and make them a part of your production.

If making *relishes*, *pickles or other preserves*, it is best to use proper preserving jars. It is difficult to make sure that jars with screw-on lids or plastic wrap tops are totally airtight, and the liquid in these preserves would obviously escape much more easily than jelly or jam. Also, you should never put anything containing vinegar in a jar with an uncoated metal screw-on lid, as the metal can react with the vinegar and makes the preserve go brown. It probably wouldn't do you any harm but doesn't look very appetizing! (This doesn't apply to chutney, however, if you seal it with a waxed disc or paraffin wax.) It would be all right to put a fairly solid chutney in a jar with a plastic wrap lid, but obviously hazardous to put a pickle with a lot of liquid in such a container, as the puncturing of the top could easily mean disaster.

The most expensive preserving jars are probably the most reliable. These come in two styles. The first has a lid comprised either of a coated metal disc, rimmed in rubber on the inside, or a clear glass disc around which you suspend a rubber ring. The metal version has a metal screw-on band and the glass version a plastic one which overlaps the disc at the top and, when screwed on firmly, makes the jar airtight. The metal disc should be used only once in preserving; in the case of the glass top, the rubber ring should also be used only once before replacement when pickling. They can be used several times before replacement when making jams or jellies. The metal screw-on band is also replaceable should it begin to deteriorate.

The second kind of jar works on very much the same principle, but its top is glass, held to the body of the jar by metal clips and made airtight by a rubber ring, which should again be changed with each use.

Price is the only factor that gives cause for thought in using either kind – and in the pickling season you may have a hard time getting just the sizes you want as they get sold out quickly. If I were certain that everyone I gave food presents to would return the jars, I would always use proper preserving jars, but alas this is not always the case, particularly if giving food presents to faraway friends.

Labels: should be big enough to accommodate easily and neatly the contents and date of making, but not so big as to make putting them on difficult. Self-adhesive labels are easiest to use (see general notes on labelling, p. 16).

Equipment

A *preserving pan* (looks like a big saucepan, usually made of heavy gauge aluminium, with loop handles on each side) isn't a necessity, but really is the best thing to make preserves in. Try to find one with a lip, which aids pouring greatly. Alternatively, you can use a big heavy-bottomed saucepan. Aluminium is advisable as it does not affect flavour and should be heavy gauge to discourage burning. Never make jam or jelly in ironware as fruit acids react with iron, imparting a metallic taste and dull colour. Heavy copper and stainless steel pans are fine. Jam rises significantly when cooking, so the pan must be big enough to accommodate the fruit and sugar easily and allow for a good rolling boil.

A *long-handled wooden spoon* is essential. Be sure the handle is long enough to keep the resting spoon from falling into the mixture, or has a notch to catch the side of the pan.

A *jamming funnel* is a funnel with a bottom opening of about 2 inches. The funnel sits on the top of a jar and directs the hot mixture into the jar rather than down the outside. It is a real boon in making preserves and virtually eliminates spattering. Not all ironmongers or kitchen departments have them, but a kitchen supply store ought to be able to get one for you.

A *ladle* is useful to scoop up the hot mixture from the preserving pan and a *measuring cup or jug* for easy pouring into jars.

A *jam skimmer*, which looks like a flattened ladle with a mesh insert, makes short work of skimming debris before potting.

A *sugar thermometer* makes establishing the setting point of jam and jelly easy and eliminates the need for water or cold plate setting tests.

A *jelly bag or cloth* is a necessity for all jelly-making. Bags can be bought ready-made, usually of heavy gauge linen, from kitchen supply stores, or made at home of cheese cloth or muslin, used double. About ½ yard material doubled over and lining a colander has served me well and is a lot less expensive and more movable than a ready-made jelly bag. The material can be used over and over – naturally washed in between usings – or thrown out. If you haven't a big enough colander, you can suspend the jelly bag by drawing its top edges together and fastening them to the legs of an upturned stool, allowing the bag to drip into a bowl beneath. Never squeeze a jelly bag to expedite juice as the resulting jelly will be cloudy.

Giving preserves

Giving preserves is as much a question of how much as anything else. A big jar might be just the thing for a large family but not very useful if giving to a single person. So think who you plan to give what to. I think very often it is nicest to bottle preserves in $\frac{1}{2}$ lb jars or even smaller and to give a selection of them to one person. If you put a selection of the same type and size of jar together, you get a coordinated-looking present, and it is far easier than wrapping different-sized jars.

If you save sturdy boxes – for instance, those that contain the more expensive kind of soap – you will find the tops and bottoms make excellent trays in which to set jars, surrounded by tissue paper (coloured if possible) to ensure a secure fit. Many of the trendier household stores wrap crockery and glass in coloured tissue paper, and this is worth saving for your own use. Shredded cellophane saved from other presents or crêpe paper could also be used for this purpose. The jars could also be set in foil dishes or those woven wooden or plastic baskets that berries and soft fruit are sold in. They can be stacked at the back of a cupboard until needed – but always be sure to put them away washed. If the boxes look a bit tatty, a spray with paint or enamel will cheer them up. Wallpaper samples make attractive coverings or linings for boxes as well.

When you have chosen your container the jars should be over-wrapped with transparent or coloured plastic sheets (plastic food wrap is fine for this). Place the container on 2 sheets of equal length that bisect each other, making sure they are long enough to overlap well over the tops of the jars. Secure the sheets with a ribbon, furling out the ends like in an expensive hamper.

Alternatively you could simply band 3 or 4 jars together by running sellotape, in an X shape, across the top and bottom of each jar. Turn the jars so that the labels face inward so that the tape doesn't run over them or pull them off when the package is undone. A ribbon tied in a big bow completes the wrapping.

Posting preserves

If you are planning to post preserves, I would suggest using jars made of plastic that is boilable, so that if breakage does occur in transit the jars will only be cracked and the preserve will still be usable if decanted. As glass shatters it is not advisable to trust it readily, however well packed, to the whims of the post. Do not use plastic wrap as a cover for jelly or jam being posted: the likelihood is that the elastic band of one of the jars will snap and a great gooey package will arrive. Pack the jars in a large cardboard box (see general notes on posting p. 17).

Jam and jelly sense

Fruit should always be firm, free of rotting spots, rinsed in cool water and allowed to dry before use. Over-ripe fruit does not make the best preserves as pectin and acid levels lower as fruit ripens, which affects setting and keeping properties. Half-ripe to just ripe fruit makes the best jam. As long as fruit is free of spoilage, it need not be photogenic to make jam. One often finds that plums, peaches, pears, etc., that are a bit misshapen or small are cheaper than display fruit which looks perfect for eating, and their jamming quality is just the same. This also applies to soft fruit such as strawberries, raspberries, blackberries, etc., particularly if there is more than one crop harvested in a season. The end of the season berries make splendid jam and are usually cheaper than those picked at full season. They are often picked a bit less ripe too, in order to get them harvested with summer help. Some growers allow you to pick your own berries at a reduced rate, which solves one 'what do we do this afternoon' problem. As pleaded in the introduction, make jam and jelly only in season when fruits are at their best both in flavour and value.

Hulls, pits, stones, peels: obviously, for making jam, hulls and stems of raspberries, strawberries, etc., should be removed before cooking. If you are making jelly, don't bother, since the cooked berry purée will have to be strained through a jelly bag. The hulling process will be done for you – but be sure your berries are well rinsed in cold water before cooking them. When making cherry, plum, pear, apricot or peach jam, I don't stone the fruit, and only in the case of peach do I skin it. Cooking does the work for you as the stones and pips rise to the surface to be skimmed off, and jam made with stones has a lovely slightly nutty flavour and sets better. For a more nutty flavour, crack a handful of the stones to reveal the kernel (tie stones and kernels in a piece of cheesecloth for easy removal). Other than peach skin, most fruit skin softens well and is quickly amalgamated in the jam, giving a nice texture. For smoother jam, the fruit purée can be put through a very wide mesh sieve or Mouli which will let the fruit purée through but not the peel. This should be done before adding sugar to the preserving pan. You can do the same with a fine sieve or the medium to small blade of a Mouli, when making seedless raspberry jam.

Sugar is the preservative in jams and jellies. Quantities of sugar depend on the fruit used, and they are not absolute. The more pectin there is in fruit, the more sugar it will set. As I have already said, the pectin level depends on the type of fruit and its ripeness. What you are after is the happy balance that gives a clear, bright preserve with the full flavour of the fruit, without being over-sweet, which will not turn sugary or deteriorate quickly.

Warming sugar in the oven before adding it to fruit purée or juice helps greatly in reducing shrinkage, improves the set and keeps the colour bright. I usually do this by pouring the sugar to be used into a clean roasting pan and putting it into the oven (about 250° (mark $\frac{1}{2}$) for 15 minutes).

Any white granulated sugar can be used in preserve-making, but for the best results use preserving sugar. It is not always easy to find, but is worth asking for. Preserving sugar is sugar syrup that has been processed into crystals that dissolve quickly, are less likely to burn, and produce less scum than ordinary granulated sugar (less skimming for you). If you can't find preserving sugar, use ordinary granulated sugar rather than caster, and never icing sugar. Some people prefer to use brown sugar but, to my taste, this masks the flavour of the fruit.

Pectin is the setting agent in jams and jellies. All fruit contains natural pectin – some more than others. Cooking apples, crab apples, dark-skinned plums, quinces, black and red currants, gooseberries and cranberries are high in pectin (use a scant quarter more sugar than fruit): blackberries, raspberries, fresh apricots, peaches, rhubarb and light-skinned plums have medium setting qualities (use approximately the same quantity of sugar as fruit in jam): strawberries, sweet cherries, pears, blueberries, pineapples and grapes have a low ratio of pectin, and you'll need ¾ lb (300 g) sugar for each pound (400 g) of fruit purée. You can improve the pectin level of fruit either by adding the juice of one of the high pectin fruits (about 3 tablespoons fresh lemon juice or ½ teaspoon tartaric or citric acid for every 4 lb (1600 g) fruit) or by adding a commercially produced pectin such as Certo (available at most large chemists and many food stores). Manufactured pectin comes in liquid or powdered form and the directions on the package will tell you how to adjust the cooking time. Lemon juice improves the flavour of most jam, I think, and takes care of any setting problems at the same time.

Liquid: most fruit needs only a tiny amount of water to begin cooking – just enough to keep the fruit from burning and to encourage the fruit skins to burst. Bruising the fruit a bit before cooking will also help the juices to run. Start the fruit at a low temperature until the juices run and stir well and often to keep the fruit at the bottom of the pan from burning. You can add a little water if there doesn't seem to be enough liquid.

Yields: this varies, depending on the fruit used, but basically you should get about 5 lb (2 kg) jam for every 3 lb (1200 g) seeded/stoned fruit used. This means your jam will be 60 per cent fruit, as opposed to most commercial jam which is 40 per cent, or less. Jam yields can be stretched (at the expense of flavour) by using more liquid in making and adding pectin to help set them. But surely if you are making jam to give, your aim is not to reproduce what can be bought in shops! The yield per pound of fruit is less for jelly than for jam, but is less easy to calculate as it depends on the juiciness of the fruit used.

Setting points: if you have a sugar thermometer, use it. 220°F is jam and jelly setting point. Testing for setting can also be done by dropping a bit of jam or jelly on a cold plate and allowing it to cool. (When testing for set, be sure to remove the preserving pan from the heat as well, to avoid overcooking.) When the blob of cooled jam or jelly wrinkles at the push of your finger, a set has been obtained.

Most jam, but particularly strawberry and cherry, needs to

rest in the pan for about 20 minutes before potting. This keeps the fruit pieces in the jam from rising to the top of the jars when cooled.

Sealing: once the jam or jelly is potted, you must seal the jars with as little airspace as possible. It should either be sealed hot, as it is poured into the jars, or quite cold. Never seal jam or jelly that is lukewarm, as it will be more likely to ferment or go mouldy.

Either a thin layer of melted paraffin or a waxed sealing disc will keep air from touching the top of the jam, followed, of course, by either the lid of the jar securely screwed on or a covering of plastic wrap secured with an elastic band. Sealing discs are usually available in stationery shops in sets with precut jam pot covers, but they are easy to make oneself. Cut a pattern of the top opening of jars to be used and cut discs out of waxed paper. Lay the discs on top of the potted jam or jelly and press gently to remove air bubbles. I prefer waxed discs to paraffin as they are easier to remove and one does not have to deal with melting paraffin, but the result is the same. Paraffin used in preserving is very like candle wax. It can be bought in household departments, then melted and poured on top of the potted jam or jelly. Use an empty fruit juice tin, with one end removed, to melt the paraffin in and you won't ruin a saucepan. Do not disturb jars until the contents are set and cooled. Recheck that lids are on securely, and wipe over to remove any spills, before labelling and storing.

Disaster areas

I hope you don't have to consult this section, simply taking heart to know it is here if you need it.

If your jam or jelly is runny, it lacks pectin. Decant back into the preserving pan (rewashing and sterilizing jars, discarding waxed discs, washing and remelting paraffin etc.) and add fresh lemon juice or commercial pectin and reboil quickly until setting occurs. Reheating cooled jam or jelly that hasn't set properly is a necessity at times, but not wildly desirable, so keep the reboiling to a minimum to retain as much of the flavour and colour as possible.

If the top of the jam or jelly becomes covered in mould, you probably haven't sealed the jars properly, or have used wet, cold jars or have sealed while lukewarm. Scrape off mould (if deepset, throw the lot out), reboil and pot properly.

If jam or jelly becomes sugary, it needs more acid. Decant and reboil with a healthy slug of lemon juice. Sugariness can still be caused by the mixture being boiled before all the sugar has melted, by constant stirring when boiling, by insufficient sealing, or by being kept at a very low temperature when stored.

Fermentation can be caused by insufficient boiling, too little sugar or storage in a wet, warm place. If you catch this early, decant and boil quickly.

If more than one of the above happens to your jam or jelly at the same time, do not try the rescue cure: count your losses and remember what you did wrong for next year.

Herb jellies

Herb jellies are wonderful accompaniments to hot or cold meat, are easily made and very colourful. I like to make them in $\frac{1}{2}$ lb jars, giving 3 or 4 different kinds together, but you could well give 1 lb jars of mint or red currant jelly. Your labels might usefully indicate what meats the jelly is recommended to accompany.

Mint jelly

This jelly is rosy red, with green bits of mint in it. I personally dislike using food colouring when making jellies that are attractively coloured in themselves and see no need to make mint jelly the screaming green it is commercially. But that, of course, is a matter of personal choice.

Yield: about 8 lb ($3\frac{1}{4}$ kg).
Keeps well: can be made in large batches to last a year.

6 lb ($2\frac{1}{2}$ kg) cooking apples, washed and quartered
2 pints (1 litre) water
1 big bunch mint, washed and bruised
2 pints (1 litre) cider vinegar
1 lb (400 g) preserving sugar for every pint ($\frac{1}{2}$ litre) of juice
1 oz (25 g) fresh mint leaves, washed and finely chopped or
$\frac{1}{2}$ oz (12 g) dried

Combine apples, water and the bunch of mint in a preserving pan. Boil until the apples are very soft. Add vinegar and boil gently for 10 minutes. Strain overnight through a jelly bag. For every pint (½ litre) of juice, add 1 lb (400 g) preserving sugar. Stir over a low heat, but do not boil until the sugar is dissolved, then boil until a set is obtained. Skim jelly well. Add chopped mint and stir through, allowing jelly to cool slightly before potting.

Damson jelly with basil

To serve with veal or poultry.

Yield: 4 to 5 lb (about 2 kg).
Keeps well.

5 lb (2 kg) damsons or cooking plums, washed
2½ pints (1¼ litres) water
2 oz (50 g) fresh basil leaves, washed, or 1 oz (25 g) dried
1 lb (400 g) preserving sugar for every pint (½ litre) of juice
1 oz (25 g) fresh basil leaves, washed and chopped, or ½ oz
   (12 g) dried

In a large preserving pan, combine plums, water and the 2 oz (50 g) basil leaves. Boil together until the plums are pulpy and soft. Strain overnight through a jelly bag. For every pint (½ litre) of juice obtained, add 1 lb (400 g) preserving sugar. Stir over a low heat, without boiling, until the sugar is dissolved, then boil until a set is obtained. Skim and add the chopped basil, allowing jelly to rest for about 5 minutes before potting.

Crab apple and chive jelly

To serve with cold meat.

Yield: 6 to 8 lb (about 3 kg).
Keeps well.

6 lb (2½ kg) crab apples, washed and halved
2 pints (1 litre) water
1½ oz (37 g) fresh chives, washed and snipped, or ¾ oz (18 g)
   freeze-dried
6 cloves
1 pint (½ litre) cider vinegar
1 lb (400 g) preserving sugar for every pint (½ litre) of juice

Combine crab apples, water, half of the chives, and cloves in a large preserving pan and boil together until crab apples are soft. Add vinegar and boil for another 5 minutes. Strain overnight through a jelly bag. For every pint ($\frac{1}{2}$ litre) of juice, add 1 lb (400 g) preserving sugar. Stir over a low heat, but do not boil, until the sugar dissolves, then boil until a set is obtained. Skim and add remaining chives, allowing jelly to rest for 5 minutes before potting.

Tomato jelly with basil and tarragon

To serve with cold meat.

Yield: About 4 lb ($1\frac{1}{2}$ kg).
Keeps well, but make in small batches as jelly tends to cloud after 6 months.

$\frac{1}{2}$ pint ($\frac{1}{4}$ litre) basil and tarragon infusion (see method)
1 pint ($\frac{1}{2}$ litre) tomato juice
3 lb (1200 g) preserving sugar
$3\frac{1}{2}$ tablespoons lemon juice
1 level tablespoon celery seed, tied in a piece of muslin
1 bottle Certo (pectin)
1 oz (25 g) fresh basil and tarragon leaves, washed and
  chopped, or $\frac{1}{2}$ oz (12 g) dried

Make infusion by combining 2 oz (50 g) washed mixed fresh basil and tarragon leaves (1 oz (25 g) dried) in 1 pint ($\frac{1}{2}$ litre) water. Bring to the boil and boil gently until reduced by half. Strain through muslin.

Combine infusion, tomato juice, preserving sugar, lemon juice and celery seed in a large pan. Stir constantly over a low heat, without boiling, to dissolve sugar, then bring to the boil. Add Certo. Return to the boil, removing celery seed and adding chopped herbs. Rest for 5 minutes before potting.

Sage and apple jelly

To serve with pork and duck.

Yield: 6 to 8 lb (about 3 kg).
Keeps well, can be made in large batches to last a year.

6 lb (2½ kg) cooking apples, washed and quartered
juice and rind of 2 lemons
water to cover (about 3 pints (1½ litres))
1 lb (400 g) preserving sugar for every pint (½ litre) of juice
2 oz (50 g) fresh sage leaves, washed, or 1 oz (25 g) dried
1 oz (25 g) fresh sage leaves, washed and chopped, or ½ oz
    (12 g) dried and crumbled (don't use powdered sage as it
    does not distribute well in jelly)

Combine apples, lemon juice and rind, water and 2 oz (50 g)
fresh sage leaves in a large preserving pan. Boil gently until the
apples are very soft. Strain through a jelly bag overnight. For
each pint (½ litre) of juice, add 1 lb (400 g) preserving sugar.
Stir over a low heat, without boiling, until the sugar is dissolved,
then boil until a set is obtained. Skim if necessary and add the
chopped sage. Allow to rest for 5 minutes before potting.

Red currant and marjoram jelly

To serve with veal or pork.

Yield: 4 to 5 lb (about 2 kg).
Keeps well.

3 lb (1200 g) red currants, washed, leaving stalks on
1 pint ($\frac{1}{2}$ litre) water
2 oz (50 g) fresh marjoram washed, or 1 oz (25 g) dried
1 lb (400 g) preserving sugar for each pint ($\frac{1}{2}$ litre) of juice
1 oz (25 g) fresh marjoram, washed and chopped, or $\frac{1}{2}$ oz
  (12 g) dried

Combine currants, water and the 2 oz (50 g) marjoram in a preserving pan. Boil gently until the currants are very soft. Strain overnight through a jelly bag and add 1 lb (400 g) preserving sugar for each pint ($\frac{1}{2}$ litre) of juice. Stir over a low heat, without boiling, until sugar is dissolved, then boil until a set is obtained. Skim if necessary and add chopped marjoram. Allow to rest for 5 minutes before potting.

Parsley and oregano jelly

To serve with veal or chicken.

Yield: about 8 lb ($3\frac{1}{4}$ kg).
Keeps well; should be made about 2 months before giving as flavour improves.

6 lb ($2\frac{1}{2}$ kg) cooking apples, washed and quartered
2 pints (1 litre) water
2 oz (50 g) fresh parsley, washed – this recipe should only be
  made with fresh
1 oz (25 g) fresh oregano washed, or $\frac{1}{2}$ oz (12 g) dried
1 pint ($\frac{1}{2}$ litre) wine vinegar
1 pint ($\frac{1}{2}$ litre) tarragon vinegar
1 lb (400 g) preserving sugar for every pint ($\frac{1}{2}$ litre) of juice
1 oz (25 g) mixed chopped fresh parsley and oregano

Combine apples, water, parsley and oregano in a preserving pan. Boil gently until apples are very soft. Add vinegars and boil for another 10 minutes. Strain overnight through a jelly bag. For every pint ($\frac{1}{2}$ litre) of juice, add 1 lb (400 g) preserving sugar. Stir over a low heat, without boiling, until the sugar is dissolved, then boil until a set is obtained. Skim if necessary and add chopped herbs. Allow to rest for 5 minutes before potting.

Lemon verbena jelly

Lemon verbena is one of the herbs grown particularly for its heady bouquet. Dried verbena leaves are available from most herbalists. Serve with cold meat.

Yield: 6 lb ($2\frac{1}{2}$ kg).
Keeps well.

6 lb ($2\frac{1}{2}$ kg) cooking apples, washed and quartered
3 pints ($1\frac{1}{2}$ litres) water
1 lb (400 g) preserving sugar for every pint ($\frac{1}{2}$ litre) of juice
rind of 1 lemon, tied in a muslin bag for easy removal
1 handful fresh lemon verbena leaves, washed, tied in a muslin
   bag; half that quantity if using dried verbena.

Combine apples and water in a large preserving pan. Boil until apples are very soft. Strain overnight through a jelly bag. Add 1 lb (400 g) preserving sugar for every pint ($\frac{1}{2}$ litre) of juice. Stir over a low heat without boiling, until sugar has dissolved, then add lemon rind and verbena leaves. Boil until a set is obtained. Remove lemon rind and verbena leaves. Skim if necessary and pot.

Basil and orange jelly

To serve with poultry.

Yield: 4 to 5 lbs (about 2 kg).
Keeps moderately well, but will cloud somewhat after 6 months.

$\frac{1}{2}$ pint ($\frac{1}{4}$ litre) basil infusion (see method)
$\frac{3}{4}$ pint (375 ml) orange juice, fresh or reconstituted frozen
$\frac{1}{4}$ pint (125 ml) water
$\frac{1}{4}$ pint (125 ml) fresh lemon juice
3 lb (1200 g) preserving sugar
1 bottle Certo (pectin)
1 oz (25 g) fresh basil leaves, washed and chopped, or $\frac{1}{2}$ oz
   (12 g) dried

Make basil infusion by combining 2 oz (50 g) washed fresh basil leaves (1 oz (25 g) dried) with a pint of water. Bring to the boil and boil until reduced by half. Strain through muslin.

Combine basil infusion, orange juice, water and lemon juice in a large saucepan. Add preserving sugar. Stir over a low heat, without boiling, until sugar is completely dissolved, then bring to the boil and add Certo. Return to the boil. Remove from heat and add chopped basil. Allow to rest for 5 minutes before potting.

Cranberry jelly with thyme

To serve with poultry.

Yield: 4 to 5 lb (about 2 kg).
Keeps well.

3 lb (1200 g) cooking apples, washed and quartered
2 lb (800 g) fresh or frozen cranberries, washed and picked over
1 oz (25 g) fresh thyme leaves, washed and bruised, or ½ oz
   (12 g) dried
water to cover fruit
1 lb (400 g) preserving sugar for each pint (½ litre) of juice
½ oz (12 g) fresh thyme leaves, washed and chopped or
   ¼ oz (6 g) dried

Combine apples, cranberries, 1 oz (25 g) thyme leaves and water in a large preserving pan. Boil gently until fruit is soft. Strain overnight through a jelly bag. For each pint (½ litre) of juice, add 1 lb (400 g) preserving sugar. Stir over a low heat, without boiling, until sugar is dissolved, then boil until a set is obtained. Skim if necessary and add the chopped thyme leaves. Allow to rest for 5 minutes before potting.

Jams, etc.

Damson jam with walnuts

Small, dark plums are best for making this jam with; they should be ripe but firm.

Yield: 8 lb (3¼ kg).
Keeps very well.

5 lb (2 kg) plums, washed and stems removed
1 lb (400 g) seedless raisins
8 oz (200 g) walnut halves or pieces
5 lb (2 kg) preserving sugar
juice and grated rind of 2 oranges
juice and grated rind of 2 lemons

Bruise the plums a bit to help the juices run. Remove any stones that come easily to hand (the rest will be removed after cooking), then combine all ingredients except walnuts in a preserving pan. Stir through and leave overnight. Put the pan over a low flame and cook, stirring to keep the jam from sticking, until the mixture is thick, but do not boil until the sugar is completely dissolved. Test for set, skim off any scum and free stones, add walnuts, and pot.

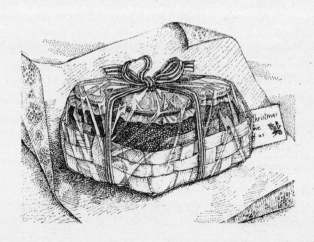

Lemon jam

Although the ingredients are the same as for marmalade, this jam has a fresh light flavour and soft colour. Choose thin-skinned lemons, and as clean and firm as possible, as the brightness of the jam depends on this. Seedless lemons will save you having to skim pips later.

Yield: 12 to 13 lb (about 5 kg).
Keeps 6 months: thereafter tends to darken.

4 lb (1600 g) lemons
5 pints (2½ litres) water
6 lb (2½ kg) preserving sugar

Wash lemons and cut off any stem ends and blemishes. Roughly cut lemons up into 6 or 8 pieces each and combine with water in a preserving pan. Cover and bring to a gentle boil, cooking until the lemon rind is soft. Uncover and add sugar, stirring without boiling, until it has completely dissolved. Boil gently, as you want the jam as light-coloured as possible, stirring well. In about 15 minutes the jam should be thickening: remove pan from heat and test for a soft set. You do not want a firm set, so it is important not to boil jam for any longer than is necessary. Soft set obtained, skim off any pips that have come to the surface, and process or chop the rough jam coarsely so bits of it are quite distinct. Return mixture to the preserving pan. It will probably be lumpy. With the back of a wooden spoon, mash the lumps against the side of the preserving pan to produce a fairly uniform smooth jam. Return pan to a low heat and stir constantly (at this stage, the jam will burn very easily) just until it bubbles. Remove from heat and pot in the usual way.

Orange and apricot marmalade

This is a marvellous tangy and rich marmalade. Seville oranges are recommended, but if they are not available use thick-skinned oranges, as bitter as possible.

Yield: 6 lb (2½ kg).
Keeps very well.

2 lb (800 g) oranges
1 large lemon
6 oz (150 g) dried apricots, washed and finely chopped
2 pints (1 litre) water
4 lb (1600 g) preserving sugar

Scrub oranges and lemon, cut into quarters (reserving pips) and roughly chop. Tie pips in a piece of clean cloth. Put all fruit and pips in a preserving pan, cover with the water and leave overnight to soak.

Bring fruit to the boil gently, uncovered, for about 1½ hours, by which time the peel should be tender. The cooking time required will depend on the kind of oranges you use, so keep an eye on the pan. When the peel is tender, remove the bag of pips, and take the pan from the heat.

Add sugar, stirring constantly without boiling, until it is completely dissolved. Bring marmalade to the boil and boil for about 20 minutes, stirring only to keep the peel from sticking. Test for set. Allow to rest for 20 minutes before potting.

Pear and ginger jam

When pears are plentiful and cheap in the late summer and autumn it is time to make this jam which I like for the bite the ginger gives. Choose under-ripe pears.

Yield: 4 lb (about 1½ kg).
Keeps well.

1½ lb (600 g) pears, peeled, cored and roughly chopped
3 lb (1200 g) preserving sugar
juice and rind of 4 lemons
8 oz (200 g) crystallized ginger, chopped

Combine all ingredients in a large bowl and leave, covered, for at least 24 hours. Stir occasionally.

Decant into a preserving pan and cook over medium heat, stirring to prevent burning, until the pears are soft, but do not boil until the sugar is completely dissolved. Then bring to a rolling boil and allow to boil until a set is obtained and the jam is ready to pot.

Lemon and marrow jam

This is a kind of lemon curd, and to my mind infinitely preferable. Country cooks have long known what splendid jam
marrow makes, and marrow combined with lemon produces a
greeny-yellow textured jam, full of lemon flavour but without
the oppressive richness from which lemon curd often suffers.
Use only unblemished, clean lemons, thin-skinned if possible.
Huge, mature marrows work best.

Yield: about 4 lb (1½ kg).
Keeps moderately well. Best consumed within three months of
making.

2 lb (800 g) peeled, seeded marrow (about 3 lb whole marrow)
  cut up
2 large lemons, seeded and roughly cut up
2 lb (800 g) granulated sugar
4 oz (100 g) butter

Cook the marrow in a very little water, covered. When soft,
drain thoroughly pressing down in a sieve to extract as much
water as possible.

In a food processor (or food mill on medium blade), combine the cooked marrow and the cut-up lemons. Process to
produce a uniform mush, with tiny pieces of lemon rind all
through it.

In a heavy-bottomed biggish saucepan, combine the lemon/
marrow mixture, the sugar and butter. Stir constantly over a
low heat until the butter and sugar are melted, bring to the boil
and simmer until nicely thickened. This should not take very
long, but the cooking time will depend on the juiciness of the
lemons and how much moisture you have extracted from the
marrow. Watch closely while boiling, as you do not want the
jam to colour or burn. Remove from heat, skim if necessary and
pot as usual.

Variation: try a mixture of citrus fruits – lime is particularly
nice.

Pickles and relishes

Apple butter

Apple butter is a traditional American recipe and is somewhere between chutney and jam. Thick and spicy, it is marvellous with cold meat, but equally so with bread and butter.

Yield: about 5 lb (2 kg).
Keeps exceptionally well, although it will shrink a bit in the jars if you keep it more than a year.

3 lb (1200 g) cooking apples, washed, cored and cut up
medium cider to cover, about 2 pints (1 litre)
½ pint (¼ litre) cider vinegar
1 level tablespoon ground cinnamon
1 level tablespoon ground allspice
1 level teaspoon ground cloves
1 lb (400 g) granulated sugar or brown sugar for each pint
  (½ litre) of apple purée

Combine apples with cider and vinegar in a large saucepan and simmer until the fruit is very soft. Process until mixture is smooth and return to pan. For every pint (½ litre) of fruit purée, add 1 lb sugar and stir without boiling until the sugar is completely dissolved. Stir in spices and boil gently until the mixture thickens, stirring constantly to keep from burning. Test for set, then pot.

Corn and pepper relish

To my mind, the best relish for hamburgers. The corn, peppers and onions should remain a bit crisp and bright-coloured, the syrup thick and spicy.

Yield: about 5 lb (2 kg).
Keeps very well: will darken a bit after a year.

2 lb (800 g) corn kernels (either fresh-cut from cob or frozen)
6 large red peppers, washed, seeded and roughly chopped
6 large green peppers, washed, seeded and roughly chopped
8 Spanish onions, peeled and roughly chopped
1 pint (½ litre) cider vinegar

1 level tablespoon salt
1½ lb (600 g) sugar
2 level tablespoons whole mustard seed
1 level tablespoon whole cloves, heads removed

If using frozen corn, allow it to thaw before use. Blanch vegetables, drain and set aside. Combine vinegar, salt, sugar and spices in a preserving pan and boil rapidly to form a light syrup, about 5 minutes. Turn vegetables into syrup and bring mixture to the boil. Pack into hot, sterilized jars and fill to overflowing with syrup, then seal.

Cranberry and orange relish

Tart, sweet and a change from cranberry sauce, this relish can also be used as a jam. Goes well with all poultry, especially turkey.

Yield: about 4 lb (1½ kg).
Keeps very well.

½ pint (¼ litre) water
1 lb (400 g) dark soft brown sugar
8 oz (200 g) granulated sugar
½ pint (¼ litre) cider vinegar
2 level teaspoons powdered cloves
2 cinnamon sticks
2 oranges, washed, seeded and coarsely chopped
2 lb (800 g) whole fresh cranberries, washed and picked over

Combine all ingredients except fruit in a preserving pan and boil together rapidly to make a light syrup, about 5 minutes. Reduce heat to medium and turn in fruit. Cook, stirring constantly, until the cranberries begin to pop, remove cinnamon sticks, then pot.

Variation: for a special flavour, pour 1½ tablespoons brandy into the preserving pan over the boiling fruit and stir through once before potting.

Beetroot relish

This is a marvellously adaptable relish, devotees of which tell me it is also wonderful as jam. I like it served with cold, bland meat such as pork.

Yield: 8 lb (3¼ kg).
Keeps very well, although the colour will darken a bit after 6 months.

5 lb (2 kg) raw beetroot, washed and peeled
3½ lb (1400 g) granulated sugar
3 oz (75 g) ginger root (fresh preferred) finely diced
juice and finely grated rind of 4 lemons
8 oz (200 g) blanched almonds, slivered

Put the beetroot through a mincer using the coarsest blade. Just cover with water and simmer in a heavy saucepan until tender. This should take the best part of an hour. Add sugar, ginger and lemon rind and juice. Remove from heat when sugar is dissolved and stir in slivered almonds, then pot.

Horseradish and beetroot relish

This is a splendid, crisp relish with a sharp flavour and a deep ruby colour. Goes well with hot beef and most cold meats.

Yield: 2 lb (800 g).
Keeps well, but colour will fade after about 3 months, so make in small quantities near to the time of giving.

1 lb (400 g) raw beetroot, washed and peeled
8 oz (200 g) fresh horseradish (half this quantity of dried can
  be used, but it is inferior to fresh)
pinch of salt
good pinch of sugar
cider or onion vinegar to cover

Cook beetroot until it is just cooked but still rather crisp. Coarsely grate beetroot and horseradish. Mix in salt and sugar and pack into hot, sterilized jars. Fill to overflowing with vinegar and seal.

Apple and orange chutney

This goes well with cold poultry or pork. Choose big, thin-skinned oranges.

Yield: 8 lb (3¼ kg).
Keeps very well.

2 oranges, sliced and seeded
4 lb (1600 g) cooking apples, washed, cored and roughly
  chopped
1 lb (400 g) sultanas
1 level teaspoon ground cloves
1 level teaspoon ground nutmeg
1 lb (400 g) onions, peeled and roughly chopped
2 lb (800 g) sugar
1½ pints (¾ litre) cider vinegar
8 oz (200 g) chopped walnuts

Combine all ingredients except walnuts in a preserving pan and cook, covered, over a medium heat until the juices of the fruit run well and the apples are soft. Uncover and stir from time to time until the mixture is thick and the peel soft. Process the chutney or use a mincer, using the coarsest blade (it should have some texture and not be completely smooth). Return to preserving pan and bring to the boil. Remove from heat, stir in walnuts and pot.

Plum and raisin chutney

This is a wonderful purple chutney that is fairly spicy. It goes well with ham and other cured meats. You should use red or purple plums.

Yield: 6 lb (2½ kg).
Keeps very well.

4 lb (1600 g) plums washed and stoned
1 lb (400 g) cooked apples, washed and cored
2 cloves garlic, pressed
3 dried chillies
1 lb (400 g) seedless raisins

2 pints (1 litre) cider vinegar
1 level tablespoon ground ginger
1 level teaspoon ground allspice
1½ lb (600 g) light soft brown sugar

Combine all ingredients except sugar in a preserving pan. Bring to the boil and cook uncovered for about 15 minutes, stirring occasionally. Add sugar and stir constantly until it has dissolved. Gently boil mixture until it thickens, which should be about 30 minutes. If you like a smooth chutney, process briefly or use a mincer with the coarsest blade; otherwise pot as it is. If you are making a smooth chutney, bring back to the boil briefly after processing before potting.

Chilli sauce

Chilli sauce may not sound like a very alluring present, but this sauce bears little resemblance to the bottled kind, and is one of the most useful items in my kitchen, quite at home for use as a chutney, barbecue sauce or sandwich spread with cheese. It has a strong flavour and lovely aroma and can be made mild or very hot depending on the amount of chillies you use.

Yield: about 8 lb (3¼ kg).
Keeps almost indefinitely, its flavour mellowing with time.

2 lb (800 g) cooking apples, washed, cored and coarsely
  chopped
2 lb (800 g) ripe tomatoes, washed and coarsely chopped
2 lb (800 g) onions, peeled and coarsely chopped
4 cloves garlic, pressed
1 lb (400 g) sultanas
1 lb (400 g) dark soft brown sugar
1 level tablespoon mustard seed ⎤
1 level tablespoon whole allspice ⎬ tied together in a muslin bag
1 level tablespoon whole cloves ⎦
6 whole dried chillies (more if you like very hot chutneys),
  tied in a muslin bag
1 level tablespoon salt
2 pints (1 litre) cider vinegar

Combine all ingredients in a big preserving pan and simmer gently over a medium heat until the mixture is thick. Stir occasionally to keep sauce from sticking. When thick and no liquid runs around the edge of the sauce in the pan, remove from heat and allow to cool for 15 minutes. Remove spice bag and discard; remove chilli bag and keep. Process the cool chilli sauce or mince, using the coarsest blade, and taste. If it is not spicy enough for your taste, put one chilli from those you have removed through your mincer and add to sauce. Taste after each addition until the mixture is spicy enough. Return sauce to the heat and bring just to the boil. Stir through once and pot.

Pickled peaches

These are a marvellous accompaniment to cold ham, turkey or chicken. Choose peaches that are on the small side: they fit the jars better with less cutting up and are generally cheaper than big dessert peaches. The peaches should also be slightly under-ripe.

Yield: about 6 lb (2½ kg).
Keep well, but preferably in the dark, as the peaches tend to darken when kept in light conditions. Should be made at least 2 months before giving.

2 lb (800 g) sugar
1 pint (½ litre) cider vinegar
15 whole cloves, heads removed
2 cinnamon sticks
8 oz (200 g) sultanas, washed and plumped in 8 tablespoons cider vinegar
rind of 1 big lemon, cut in ½-inch strips ⎤ tied in a piece of
1 level teaspoon whole allspice ⎦ muslin
5 lb (2 kg) peaches

Combine all ingredients except peaches in a preserving pan, stirring over a medium heat until the sugar is completely dissolved, then boil rapidly for 3 minutes and take off heat.

Peel peaches (best done by covering a few at a time in boiling water to loosen skins), remove stones and cut into thickish slices, dropping them into the vinegar and sugar mixture. When all the peaches are sliced, return preserving pan to heat and allow to come to the boil. With a slotted spoon, remove peaches, and pack into hot, sterilized jars. Fish out cinnamon sticks, lemon rind and allspice from vinegar. Divide sultanas evenly between jars and allow a couple of cloves per jar as well. Fill jars to overflowing with vinegar mixture. Depress fruit with the back of a spoon to release trapped air and top up with vinegar and sugar mixture. Seal.

Pickled orange rings

This is a very pretty pickle, whose colour and flavour improves cold meat, particularly fowl or game, immensely. Be sure to choose seedless oranges; the smaller size ones keep their shape better and disintegrate less in cooking than big ones.

Yield: about 3 lb (1¼ kg).
Keep very well.

8 oranges
1½ pints (¾ litre) cider vinegar
2 lb (800 g) sugar
1 level tablespoon whole cloves, heads removed
3 cinnamon sticks

Wash oranges and slice into pieces ¼ inch thick. Put them into a preserving pan and barely cover with water. Simmer gently until the peel begins to soften, about 30 minutes. Take care not to boil hard as the oranges will turn into a pulpy mass. With a slotted spoon remove oranges to a plate. Add all other ingredients to the water the oranges have been cooking in. Boil hard for 10 minutes and then reduce heat. Slip the orange slices back into the preserving pan and bring mixture back to the boil. Remove orange slices with a slotted spoon and pack into hot, sterilized jars. Boil the remaining syrup until it begins to thicken, then fill jars to overflowing with it, allowing a few cloves to drift into each jar, but not the cinnamon. Depress fruit with the back of a spoon to release trapped air, top up jars with syrup and seal.

Pickled grapes

This pickle is best made with a mixture of black, green and red grapes. Make it when grapes are in season and cheap. Serve with ham or poultry. A very pretty pickle.

Yield: about 4 lb (1600 g).

Keep very well, although after about 9 months the grape skin becomes a bit softer than it should be. Shouldn't be used for 2 or 3 months after being made.

3 lb (1200 g) grapes, washed, picked over and stems removed
dry mustard
8 oz (200 g) sugar
1 pint (½ litre) water
4 whole cloves, heads removed
2 cinnamon sticks

Pack grapes into hot, sterilized jars (they do not need to be seeded but are even nicer if they are seeded) sprinkling each layer with dry mustard; about 1 level teaspoon per layer is about right. You may want to fiddle the grapes around a bit to fit as many as possible into the jar. Combine sugar, water, cloves and cinnamon in a saucepan and boil together until a syrup forms. Remove from heat, remove cinnamon sticks and pour over grapes filling jars to overflowing. Allow 1 clove per jar. Depress fruit with the back of a spoon to release trapped air, top up jars with syrup and seal.

Bitter lemon pickle

The flavour of this pickle defies specific description, and I'll admit the combination of ingredients does seem a bit strange, but the result is terrific. Serve with cold meat. Choose thin-skinned lemons, seedless if possible.

Yield: about 5 lb (2 kg).
Keeps well: make 2 months before you want to give.

8 lemons
2 level tablespoons salt
1 lb (400 g) sultanas, chopped
1 tablespoon chopped fresh ginger
1 level teaspoon chilli powder
4 cloves of garlic, pressed
$\frac{1}{2}$ pint ($\frac{1}{4}$ litre) cider vinegar
$1\frac{1}{2}$ lb (600 g) light soft brown sugar
2 level teaspoons grated horseradish, fresh if possible

Wash lemons and slice (discarding any pips) into eight pieces lengthways. Sprinkle with salt and keep in the fridge for at least 36 hours, stirring from time to time. Drain and reserve liquid. Put the lemons through a mincer, using the coarsest blade, and combine with the reserved lemon liquid and all the other ingredients in a big saucepan. Simmer over a low heat until the mixture is thick. Pot.

Pickled mushrooms

These are splendid accompaniments to cold meat, in salads or on toothpicks as an hors d'oeuvre. The small button mushrooms are neater and prettier than big, flat field mushrooms, but do not have nearly the flavour of the less tidy ones.

Yield: about 4 lb ($1\frac{1}{2}$ kg).
Keep well.

3½ lb (1400 g) mushrooms, dry bits of stem removed
1 level tablespoon salt
2 Spanish onions, thinly sliced
1½ pints (¾ litre) tarragon vinegar
1 level tablespoon cayenne pepper
1 level teaspoon celery seed
sprigs of fresh tarragon (optional)

Wipe or wash the mushrooms, depending how dirty they are but be sure they are well dried before starting to pickle. If using big mushrooms, quarter them, leaving some stem with each piece. Sprinkle liberally with salt and leave them on a flat serving plate that will accommodate them easily. After about 30 minutes, turn the mushrooms and salt into a medium saucepan and put over a low heat until the mushrooms wilt and begin to release their liquid. Add all other ingredients except fresh tarragon and simmer gently for 10 minutes. Pack mushrooms and onions into hot, sterilized jars. Return liquid to heat and bring to the boil. Fill jars to overflowing with liquid; depress contents with the back of a spoon to release trapped air. Pop in sprig of tarragon, top up jars with liquid and seal.

Pickled onions

Not being a devotee of malt vinegar, I tried making pickled onions with red wine vinegar, and the result was such a success that friends started inquiring about my pickled onion production as soon as pickling onions appeared on the market. Choose small yellow pickling onions, small white onions or shallots.

Yield: about 3 lb (1¼ kg).
Keep very well, but should be made at least a month before giving.

2 lb (800 g) onions
1½ level tablespoons salt
3 dried chillies
whole tarragon leaves (dried are fine, but fresh for preference)
6 whole cloves, heads removed
1 pint (½ litre) red wine vinegar
6 oz (150 g) sugar

Trim off the top and roots of the onions carefully – as little as possible of the onion itself should be removed. Put trimmed onions in a deep bowl and cover with boiling water. After 1 minute, pour off water and the skins of the onions will come away quite easily. Use a sharp knife and peel onions, under running cold water. Sprinkle skinned onions with salt and leave overnight. Rinse thoroughly and roll onions on paper towels to remove surface moisture. Pack into hot, sterilized jars, distributing evenly. Drop a chilli, a few tarragon leaves and 2 cloves into each jar. Combine vinegar and sugar in a small saucepan and boil gently until the sugar is completely dissolved. Fill jars to overflowing; depress contents with the back of a spoon to release trapped air. Top up with vinegar and seal.

Bread and butter pickle

This is a cucumber and onion pickle with a lot of crunch to it; it got its name because it goes so well with bread and butter. Choose either pickling cucumbers or small, dark-skinned, completely firm salad cucumbers. The smaller the cucumber, the smaller the ratio of seeds to flesh it is likely to contain, and it is the firm flesh of the cucumber that you are after, since the seedy part will get a bit slimy after a couple of months in a vinegar bath. Slices of small cucumbers fit pickling jars best.

Yield: about 3 lb (1¼ kg).
Keeps well; colour will fade after 6 months, but taste is unaffected by keeping. Should be made a month before giving.

2 9-inch cucumbers, unpeeled
1½ lb (600 g) Spanish onions
2 level tablespoons salt
1 pint (½ litre) white wine or tarragon vinegar
6 oz (150 g) sugar
1 level teaspoon celery seed
1 level teaspoon whole mustard seed

Wash cucumbers, dry and slice into ⅛-inch slices. Peel onions and slice into ⅛-inch slices, then cut across the slices to break them up. Combine cucumber and onions in a deep bowl and toss gently with salt. Leave for 1 hour and then drain in a colander, but do not rinse. Pack into hot, sterilized jars.

Heat vinegar, sugar and spices in a saucepan until the sugar is dissolved. Pour over the cucumber and onion, filling jars to overflowing and allowing some celery and mustard seed to drift into each jar. Depress contents with the back of a spoon to release trapped air. Top up and seal.

Watermelon pickle

To my mind, you just can't beat watermelon pickle for flavour and crunch. Any melon rind will make good pickles, but watermelon rind is the only one that maintains the crunch so characteristic of this pickle. Serve with cold beef or ham.

It is a bit hard to give an accurate assessment of how much pickle this recipe yields since this will depend on the thickness of the rind. There is a fair amount of peeling (alas no short cut for melons) and cutting up, so I suggest you start with 1 watermelon weighing 6–8 lb (about 3 kg) and see how much you get from it before buying melons in quantity. Have a party to consume the red flesh of the watermelon, as you don't use it for this pickle.

For the uninitiated, watermelons come in either of 2 varieties: the football-sized, dark, green-skinned variety, or the big, oblong variety which has either a dark green skin or a lightish mottled green skin. Beneath the skin is a greenish white rind and then the red flesh with a lot of seeds that one eats.

Keeps well, but needs to be kept in a dark place to preserve the colour.

6–8 lb (about 3 kg) watermelon
2 level tablespoons salt
2 lb (800 g) sugar
2 pints (1 litre) cider vinegar
2 oranges, thinly sliced, seeded and the slices cut in half
2 lemons, thinly sliced, seeded and the slices cut in half
20 whole cloves, heads removed
4 cinnamon sticks

Cut the melon in quarters and scoop out the red flesh and seeds for consumption, but not pickle-making. I try to keep a bit of the red part of the melon attached to the white rind as it makes a more attractive pickle than the white alone. As the centre red flesh disintegrates in cooking, it is not worth trying to pickle it. With a very sharp knife, peel the dark green outside rind away, leaving as much white rind as possible. Cut the white rind into 1½-inch chunks and put into a large pan. Cover with salted water and leave in a cool place overnight. The next day, drain melon and rinse once. Set aside.

Combine the sugar and vinegar in a preserving pan and boil gently until the sugar is completely dissolved. Add oranges, lemons and spices and bring to the boil. Drop in melon rind and bring to the boil again. Remove from heat. Fish out cinnamon sticks. Pack melon, oranges and lemon slices into hot, sterilized jars. Allow 1 or 2 cloves to drift into each jar. Fill to overflowing with vinegar mixture. Depress fruit with the back of a spoon to release any trapped air and top up jars. Seal.

Piccalilli

This mustard pickle goes well with cold meats. It should be made at least three months before it is needed, as its flavours need that time to mellow.

Yield: about 8 lb (3¼ kg).
Keeps very well.

2 large (12- to 14-inch) cucumbers, seeded and cut into bite-size chunks
1½ lb (600 g) green or under-ripe tomatoes, the smaller the better
1½ (600 g) onions, peeled and sliced into thick chunks (or use pickling onions, halved if large)
1 medium head celery, cut into bite-size chunks
1 large red pepper, seeded and cut into bite-size chunks (or use one small red and one small green pepper)

Sauce
4 oz (100 g) flour, sieved
8 oz (200 g) sugar

3 level tablespoons dry mustard
1½ level teaspoons turmeric
2 level teaspoons celery seed
½ level teaspoon ground allspice
2 17.6 oz (100 cl) bottles cider or wine vinegar

Make a solution of brine by adding 4 oz of cooking salt to 1½ litres of boiled water, which has been cooled. If you are using very soft water, then you do not need to boil the water first. In a large bowl, add the cut-up cucumbers, the whole tomatoes and the onions, making sure the brine solution covers them. Set aside in a cool place overnight.

The next day, drain the vegetables well and cut up the tomatoes into firm, bite-size chunks. Add the celery and pepper to the vegetable mélange and set aside.

In a preserving pan, combine all sauce ingredients and stir over a medium heat until you have a thick, smooth sauce. If you are unlucky enough to have any flour lumps, whisk them at this point as they are virtually impossible to remove later.

To the hot sauce, add all the vegetables and stir over a medium heat to coat them and to heat through. You do not want to cook this pickle, but it must be hot before potting. Remove from heat and pack into hot, sterilized preserving jars and seal.

Variation: traditional Piccalilli includes cauliflower; use only the whitest, freshest head you can find (yellow or off-white heads tend to go grey when pickled). Cut a medium-size head into small florets and steam until barely tender. Drain and cool before adding with the celery and red pepper.

Rhubarb sultana chutney

A splendidly rich brown chutney to make in the late spring or summer when outdoor-grown rhubarb is mature. Avoid forced or spindly rhubarb; you really do want the thick, green to dark red stalks for this chutney.

Yield: 8 lb (3¼ kg).
Keeps very well.

4 lb (1600 g) rhubarb, trimmed of leaf and any dried ends,
   cut into 1½-inch lengths
1 lb (400 g) onions, peeled and roughly chopped
1 lb (400 g) sultanas
2 oranges, seeded and roughly chopped
6 dried chillies, roughly chopped
1½ pints (¾ litre) cider vinegar
2 lb (800 g) dark brown sugar
1 level teaspoon ground allspice
1 level teaspoon ground cinnamon
1 level teaspoon ground nutmeg
1 level teaspoon ground cloves

Combine the fruit, onions, chillies and vinegar in a large preserving pan and simmer until the rhubarb is cooked but not
mushy. Add brown sugar and spices, stir well, and cook over a
medium heat until thick. The vinegar should be absorbed and
very little still around the edge of the pan. Pot as usual.

Mustard pear pickle

This is a thick and spicy chutney-type pickle to make in the
autumn when pears are cheap and plentiful. Always use under-
ripe pears – windfalls are ideal.

Yield: 8 lb (3¼ kg).
Keeps very well.

5 lb (2 kg) under-ripe pears, cored and very roughly cut up
   (you want chunks)
1 lb (400 g) onions, peeled and coarsely chopped
1 lb (400 g) sultanas
2 pints (1 litre) cider vinegar
1½ lb (600 g) light soft brown sugar
1 level tablespoon salt
1 level tablespoon ground nutmeg
1 level tablespoon ground cloves
3 level tablespoons dry mustard powder, or to your own taste

Combine the pears, onions, sultanas and cider vinegar in a big
preserving pan and simmer gently over a medium heat until the

onions are translucent, but the pears firmish. You do not want the pears to disintegrate into a mass for this pickle. Add the soft brown sugar and spices, stirring to mix completely, and keep from sticking. Taste to see if you want more sugar, which may be necessary if the pears are very under-ripe. If you want a hotter pickle, add more mustard powder, remembering that the eventual pickle, having been allowed to mellow on keeping, will not be so fierce as it is when first made. Boil mixture gently and when it is thick and very little vinegar still runs around the outside of the pan, it is ready to pot. Stir through once before potting in the usual way.

Vinegars

About vinegars

A good quality, well-flavoured vinegar is much to be prized. Several varieties of flavoured vinegar can be bought in supermarkets, but they tend to be expensive and do not offer such an interesting variety of flavours as those that are easily made at home.

Vinegar should be made in relatively small quantities and not kept for many months before use, as it can and will become cloudy and form a residue at the bottom of the bottle. This is not harmful, but it isn't very attractive and can detract from the look of the food in which it is used. (See general notes on storing, p. 16.)

When making vinegar, use utensils made of glass, enamel or stainless steel. As vinegar is an acid, it has a corrosive effect on iron, copper, zinc, galvanized material, or aluminium.

If you are making flavoured vinegars in any significant quantity do try to find a store or discount wholesaler that sells the basic vinegar in large bottles, usually meant for commercial use. These will work out half the price of smaller bottles and are well worth keeping an eye out for.

Giving vinegars

Timing is important in giving vinegar as presents, as you want it at its peak of flavour, which is usually fairly soon after bottling. If you are making a herb vinegar and putting a sprig of whatever herb in it, which looks attractive, give it soon after bottling so that the herb will still be green against the amber of the vinegar, and there will be as little residue in the vinegar as possible.

I always bottle vinegar in glass or earthenware; old vinegar and olive oil bottles are recommended for this. There are plastics that work as well, but vinegar being an acid is not reliably bottled in plastic. A pint bottle looks respectable and isn't so big that it takes the recipient ages to get through. See p. 16 for general notes on labelling.

Be sure that the screw top of the bottle or cork you are using fits completely since evaporation will affect both the colour and flavour of the vinegar. To test for airtightness, fill the jar or bottle with water, screw on the lid or press in cork tightly, dry the outside of the jar and leave on the draining board upside down. If moisture escapes you would be well advised to use another cork or lid. Don't use screw-on lids made of uncoated metal, as these can react with vinegar. And if lids have cardboard liners in them be sure to remove them.

There is really no satisfactory way of posting vinegar: it is asking for trouble to post glass and vinegar can't be bottled in plastic.

Onion vinegar

This vinegar has a mellow but fresh taste and makes a fine all-purpose salad vinegar.

Yield: 2 pints (1 litre). Keeps up to 6 months without clouding.

6 Spanish onions, peeled and roughly chopped
1 level tablespoon salt
4 whole cloves
1 level tablespoon sugar
2 pints (1 litre) white vinegar, just brought to the boil

In a large jar with a wide mouth (or 2 family-size instant coffee jars) combine all ingredients and stir to blend. Seal jar and leave in a cool, dark place for 2 weeks to infuse. Strain vinegar through muslin into bottles and seal.

Garlic vinegar

The flavour of this vinegar will depend on the freshness of the garlic used.

Yield: 1½ pints (¾ litre).
Keeps well; its flavour maturing with time.

1½ pints (¾ litre) cider vinegar, just brought to the boil
3 peppercorns
3 whole cloves
12 cloves garlic, peeled and halved

Combine all ingredients in a litre bottle and seal, keeping in a cool, dark place. Taste after a week. If pungent, strain through muslin and bottle. If not strong enough, leave for another week before testing again.

Chilli pepper vinegar

This vinegar is especially recommended for use in bland salads, such as potato salad.

Yield: 1½ pints (¾ litre).
Keeps well.

1½ pints (¾ litre) white malt vinegar, just brought to the boil
3 whole cloves
3 oz (75 g) dried red chillies

Combine all ingredients in a litre bottle, seal and leave in a cool, dark place for a week to infuse, up to 2 weeks if you want vinegar to blow your head off! Strain through muslin and bottle in small quantities.

Cucumber vinegar

This vinegar is particularly good with seafood recipes.

Yield: 3 pints (1½ litres).
Keeps well.

6 cucumbers, peeled and sliced
3 Spanish onions, peeled and sliced
½ level teaspoon cayenne pepper
1 level tablespoon celery salt
2½ pints (1¼ litres) mixed cider and white malt vinegar

Combine all ingredients in a large saucepan. Bring to the boil and boil gently for two minutes. Remove from heat and allow to cool slightly. Pour mixture into 1 wide-mouthed jar or several smaller ones. Seal and leave to infuse in a cool, dark place for 10 days. Strain through muslin and bottle.

Herb vinegars

Good quality herb vinegars are easily made and greatly add flavour to salad dressings and pickles. The basic method of making tarragon, mint, thyme, marjoram or basil vinegar is as follows:

Take a litre bottle or jar which has been thoroughly washed and dried and put into it a handful of fresh herbs, collected at the peak of their flavour (just before the plant begins to flower). The herbs should be rinsed and dried on a paper towel before using. If fresh herbs aren't available, use half the quantity of whole dried herbs, trying to avoid crumbled herbs and herb dust if possible.

Fill bottle or jar with white wine, cider or white malt vinegar, seal and leave to infuse in a cool, dark place for a month. Strain through muslin or a clean tea towel into bottles and seal.

The addition of a sprig of the herb flavouring the vinegar is decorative, but the storing of such vinegar in a warm kitchen or in full light often causes clouding.

The choice of vinegar to be used is cause for experiment. My preference is white wine vinegar with tarragon and basil, cider vinegar with mint and a mixture of vinegars with thyme and marjoram. Malt vinegar has such a distinctive flavour that it can overshadow delicate herbs, and I recommend using it only in combination with other vinegars.

Mixed herb vinegar

This recipe is a particular favourite of mine and popular with friends.

Yield: about 8 pints (4 litres).
Keeps well.

8 pints (4 litres) cider vinegar
4 oz (100 g) tarragon leaves, washed, or 2 oz (50 g) dried
25 whole peppercorns
3 shallots, peeled and sliced
4 level tablespoons fresh chives, washed and snipped (2 tablespoons freeze-dried)
8 oz (200 g) mixed fresh herbs (thyme, rosemary, parsley, marjoram) washed
1 level tablespoon celery seed
1 celeriac root, scrubbed (but not peeled) and diced

Combine all ingredients and divide between several wide-mouthed jars. Seal. After 2 weeks in a cool, dark place, strain through muslin and bottle. Pop in a sprig of herb if desired before sealing.

Fruit vinegars

Fruit vinegars resemble fruit cordials, except that they are more tangy, non-alcoholic and have a number of uses. I particularly like them as a marinade for fruits for salads or 2 or 3 table-spoonfuls in a glass with ice and soda water or ginger beer on a hot day. A tablespoon or two over bland ice cream or custard makes a delightful change. Don't keep them for more than 4 months.

The best combination of fruits for fruit vinegar includes raspberries, blackberries and red or black currants. Allow 1 lb (400 g) fruit for each ½ pint (¼ litre) of vinegar. I usually use half malt and half cider vinegar.

Wash fruit and place in a glass bowl. Mash with the back of a wooden spoon and pour vinegar over fruit. Cover bowl loosely and leave mixture in a cool place for 3–5 days for flavours to infuse. Strain through muslin.

For every pint (½ litre) of juice obtained, add 1 lb (400 g) sugar. Bring to the boil in a large saucepan and boil gently for 10 minutes. Skim if necessary. Cool slightly and strain into bottles. Seal.

Potted foods

Giving potted foods

Time is again of paramount importance when planning to give potted foods. These should be given soon after making so that the recipient has the maximum amount of time to enjoy them.

Potted food can be packed in a single large container or small individual ones. Whichever you are using, always pack in crockery you don't want returned, and it will be a nice surprise if a crock is returned to you. And even if you are expecting the crock to be returned, don't use anything you are planning to use in the near future, as it may be in someone else's refrigerator when you need it.

Given the expense of using crockery to package potted food, I prefer using foil dishes; they are light to carry and I can keep a supply of them on hand. They are infinitely cheaper than even seconds of crockery, let alone easier to store, but alas not as pretty. Most stationery stores have a section with a good range of them. Another alternative is decorative plastic cups (not paper ones). If any of these containers haven't their own tops, cover with plastic wrap and fasten with ribbon or coloured elastic bands. A large dish could be overwrapped with plastic food wrap or put in a food wrap bag.

If you are giving a selection of potted foods, for instance a number of different potted cheeses, pack all the different varieties to be given in the same size containers and package them together (see p. 25 for suggestions on how to do this).

All potted foods can be frozen, though they shouldn't be kept for more than about 3 months. The terrine and potted shrimps freeze particularly well, however, as do the sausages.

See p. 16 for general notes on labelling.

Posting potted foods

If you are posting off potted foods as presents, pack them in foil dishes to avoid the possibility of cracked pots arriving: even the plastic cups could easily crack.

It is also important to remember delays in the delivery of packages if you are thinking of posting potted food, especially at Christmas time, and you should take this into consideration when deciding what to give. Obviously, if you don't have to use the post to get your gift to its recipient so much the better, but most potted foods travel well, provided their journey is not lengthy and they do not have to journey through heat for any period of time. Only post pots of cheese in fairly cold weather. When I mail potted food I always try to pack it cold, i.e. right out of the refrigerator, having put an extra layer of clarified butter over the top of pâtés, etc., to ensure that no air gets at them.

Of the following recipes, do not give sausages to anyone whom you must post to. The sausages don't contain preservative and must be kept cold or frozen, to be eaten within a day of making if not frozen. If you can keep them frozen and are giving to someone with a freezer, they are more than worth the rush from freezer to freezer. (See p. 17 for general notes on posting.)

Clarified butter is used to seal pâté. To make it, melt down unsalted butter and allow the sediment to settle. Pour off the clear liquid which is the clarified butter.

Chicken liver pâté

This is the simplest recipe for chicken liver pâté I know and probably the best. The pâté is rich, smooth and slightly gamy.

Keeps well in a refrigerator for 2 weeks covered with clarified butter.

8 oz (200 g) chicken livers (fresh or frozen and thawed), rinsed and trimmed
1 oz (25 g) butter
2 tablespoons brandy
2 level teaspoons salt
sprinkling cayenne pepper
3 oz (75 g) soft butter
clarified butter to cover (see above)

Combine livers with 1 oz (25 g) butter in a small frying pan.
Sauté the livers over a medium heat, tossing them constantly
until they are evenly browned (but not crisp or dry) on the
outside and soft and pinkish-brown on the inside.

Remove livers from the pan to a small deep bowl or bowl of a
blender. Add the brandy and seasonings to the butter in the
frying pan and heat through. Pour over the livers and add soft
butter. With the blender on low, blend until you have a smooth
paste. If mashing by hand, use the tines of a fork or potato
masher. Pack pâté into containers, smooth top and cover completely with clarified butter. Cover and refrigerate until used.

Duck pâté with water chestnuts: substitute duck for chicken
livers, port for brandy and add a few diced water chestnuts.

Venison pâté with mushrooms: substitute leftover venison for
chicken livers, and add diced mushrooms, sautéed in butter.

Chicken pâté with almonds: substitute dark meat of chicken for
chicken livers, sherry for brandy and add a few slivered almonds.

Chicken liver pâté with herbs

This pâté is made in a blender or put through a Mouli. It is rich
and fragrant with herbs.

Keeps well in the refrigerator for 2 weeks covered with clarified
butter.

8 oz (200 g) streaky bacon, diced
2 Spanish onions, peeled and sliced
1 lb (400 g) chicken livers (fresh or frozen and thawed), rinsed
    and trimmed
2 cloves garlic, pressed
4 oz (100 g) butter
salt and pepper
1 level tablespoon mixed dry herbs
3½ tablespoons red wine
2 tablespoons brandy
1 teaspoon Worcester sauce
1 tablespoon mixed French mustard (mild)
clarified butter to cover (p. 68)

Sauté the bacon and onions until the onions are transparent. Add chicken livers and garlic and toss over a medium heat until the livers are browned outside and still slightly pink inside. Remove from pan either into the bowl of a blender or to a warm plate. Add butter and all other ingredients, apart from the clarified butter, to pan and stir together over low heat until the butter is melted. If you are using a blender, add butter mixture to livers, onions and garlic in the blender bowl and blend at low speed until the mixture is smooth. If you are using a Mouli, run the livers, onions and garlic through, using the fine blade, to obtain a smooth paste, then combine them with the butter mixture, blending thoroughly before packing into containers and covering completely with clarified butter. Cover and refrigerate.

Potted game or poultry

Instead of using liver as the base for pâté, cooked game or poultry makes a welcome change and is an excellent way of using leftover duck, pheasant or venison. Infinite variety can be achieved with the addition of cooked mushrooms, groundnut meats etc. I would suggest such additions be made after you have created the basic paste. In this way you will have a lovely smooth paste accented in both texture and flavour by the addition. Use the chicken liver pâté recipe (p. 68) as a basis, substituting whatever leftover game or poultry you have for the

liver. You may want to experiment substituting rum, port, sherry or brandy. Solid meats are best reduced to paste by putting them through a food processor, in a blender, or through a Mouli using the fine blade.

A country terrine

This is a rough pâté, garlicky and delicious. It slices well.

Yield: 1 big terrine or 2 more manageable ones that should each serve 6 people as a lunch main course.

Keeps magnificently in a cool place or in the refrigerator for up to 2 weeks, its flavour improving and maturing, also freezes well.

Oven: preheated to 350° (mark 4).

1 lb (400 g) fresh pork fat
2 lb (800 g) lean pork
1 lb (400 g) pig's liver
8 oz (200 g) lamb's liver
1½ oz (37 g) butter
1 Spanish onion, peeled and finely chopped
2 cloves garlic, pressed
8 oz (200 g) chicken livers (fresh or frozen and thawed), rinsed
    and trimmed
3½ tablespoons brandy
1 egg
3½ tablespoons double cream
1½ tablespoons lemon juice
1 level tablespoon seasoned salt
1 level teaspoon grated nutmeg
½ level teaspoon cayenne pepper
4 oz (100 g) chopped ham or lean corned beef cut in cubes
8 oz (200 g) fresh pork fat or fat salt pork cut into strips
1 bay leaf

If your butcher loves you, get him to mince the pound of pork fat, pork, pig's liver and lamb's liver for you. Failing this, mince it yourself, using the medium blade of your mincer, and set aside in a big bowl. Combine butter, onion, garlic and chicken livers in a small frying pan and sauté together until the livers are browned outside, while still pinkish and soft inside. Remove livers and add brandy to the frying pan. Deglaze residue in pan, reducing it slightly and then pour over the meat mixture. Add egg, cream, lemon juice, salt, nutmeg and pepper to mixture and mix thoroughly. You can use a fork, but it is best done with your hands. Fold in chopped ham or corned beef and mix again.

Line a terrine (alternatively 2 1-lb bread tins or foil loaf tins) with the sliced pork fat so that the slices overlap and the sides and bottom of the tins are completely covered. If the strips of fat are long enough, arrange them so they can come up the sides of the dish and be wrapped over the top. If they are not long enough, line the sides and bottom and save a few strips to make a lid with.

Fill the terrine with half the pâté mixture, spreading it evenly. Arrange the chicken livers down the centre of the pâté mixture and cover with the remaining pâté. Pull the fat pork slices over the top of the pâté mixture, or arrange separate ones over the top so that it is completely covered. Impress the bay leaf on top, cover with foil and seal around the edges of the pan.

Bake the terrine in a roasting pan half-filled with water, for about 2 hours. The terrine will be cooked when the fat on top is clear and yellow.

Remove the pâté from the roasting pan and weight its top with a comparable sized terrine or loaf tin. If the pan alone is not heavy enough to do the job, fill it with 2 evenly spaced jam jars. Leave the foil over the pâté while weighting it and you will not have to wash whatever you are using as a weight. Allow the terrine to cool, completely weighted, before removing the weight and refrigerating.

Potted shrimps

Potted shrimps make a delicious and unusual present, the homemade variety being in quite a different class from the bought kind.

Keep about 2 weeks in the refrigerator, or if frozen up to 3 months, without losing their texture. The important thing to remember is that the top must be completely covered with clarified butter so that no air gets at the shrimps until they are ready to be eaten.

4 oz (100 g) butter
1 lb (400 g) shrimps or prawns, the smallest you can find,
 peeled
½ level teaspoon cayenne pepper
¼ level teaspoon ground mace
¼ level teaspoon grated nutmeg
1 teaspoon lemon juice (optional)
clarified butter to cover (p. 68)

Melt butter in a saucepan and add shrimps, seasonings and lemon juice if you are using it. Remove pan from heat and coat shrimps thoroughly. Pack shrimps into containers. They should be fairly well pressed down, but do not mash them. When cold, cover shrimp mixture with a layer of clarified butter, then cover and refrigerate.

Variation: Almost any shellfish can be made into potted sea-food, using the basic recipe for potted shrimps. If you are making potted seafood from fresh rather than tinned shellfish, make it near to the time of giving and in all cases use only top quality basic ingredients. Do not use the dark meat of crab, for although it tastes fine it looks unattractive covered with butter. If using lobster, alternate layers of lobster meat with layers of the coral, so when served you get a marbled effect which is as attractive as it is delicious. Potted salmon is also very delicious.

Smoked fish butters

For lovers of smoked fish, there can be no nicer present. Sardines, smoked mackerel, kippers and smoked salmon make fine bases. As most smoked fish is high in salt content, use unsalted butter.

Keep well for 2 weeks refrigerated.

Sardine butter: drain sardines well and mix with soft, unsalted butter in the proportion of 1 oz sardines to ½ oz butter. Add 1

teaspoon lemon juice and a sprinkling of cayenne pepper and mash the mixture thoroughly. Pack into containers and cover with clarified butter (see p. 68). Cover and refrigerate before giving.

Smoked mackerel or kipper butter: if starting with fish on the bone, i.e. not using tinned fish, cover fish with boiling water and leave for about 10 minutes. Drain and peel off skin. This should also help to remove some of the saltiness of the fish. Taste the fish at this point, and if still very salty give it another bath in boiling water. Drain thoroughly and leave the skinned fish on a paper towel to remove as much moisture as possible. Flake off flesh and proceed as for sardine butter.

Smoked salmon butter: you do not need top quality salmon for this, but avoid the grey side pieces as they look unattractive. Proceed as with sardine butter, but use the juice of $\frac{1}{2}$ lemon and omit pepper.

Taramasalata

The smoked cod's roe pâté is a favourite of mine and is certainly seen more on menus than it used to be. With its creamy texture it looks nicest packed in earthenware pots.

Keeps well, if not spectacularly, so make only a day or so before giving. It should keep for 2 weeks in the refrigerator.

6 slices white bread
8 fl oz (200 ml) milk
4 oz (100 g) smoked cod's roe (fresh or in a jar)
3 tablespoons fresh lemon juice
1 large clove garlic, pressed
7 tablespoons good quality olive oil
1 level tablespoon finely grated onion

Take the crust off the bread and soak in milk. Wring out bread until no milk comes out of it and combine bread, roe and lemon juice in a small deep bowl, or in a blender. Mash together or blend at lowest speed, adding the garlic and then the oil, drop by drop (as if you were making mayonnaise) in a thin, steady stream. Keep blending until the oil has been absorbed completely and the mixture is creamy smooth. You may find that you need a bit more olive oil to get the consistency right. Add onion. Pack into containers and refrigerate, covered.

Variation: any smoked fish roe can be substituted for the cod's roe.

Homemade sausages

Herb-rich homemade sausages are seldom found today, but they are easily made and well worth the effort. To cook, simply dust with flour and fry, browning well on both sides.

Yield: a good dozen patties.
If not frozen, be sure to use within a day of making, but they freeze well.

1½ lb (600 g) belly pork
4 oz (100 g) flat mushrooms
1 level teaspoon seasoned salt

½ level teaspoon coarsely ground pepper
1 level teaspoon paprika
½ level teaspoon garlic powder
½ level teaspoon ground nutmeg
1 level tablespoon mixed herbs (fresh if possible; use ½ oz (12 g) if dried)
1 level teaspoon chopped fresh parsley

Have the belly pork coarsely minced, either by your butcher or by you, using the coarsest blade of your mincer. Personally I think that sausages made with roughly minced pork are nicer than those with a smoother texture, but this is a matter of personal taste.

Combine all ingredients and mix well. Form into patties and freeze (if not to be used immediately) four to a pack in a stack, with a piece of foil in between each, in foil dishes or freezer-wrap.

Country sausages

These sausages are traditionally called Oxford sausages and are meatier than the first sausage recipe, without such a pronounced herb flavour. To cook, dust with flour and fry, browning well on both sides.

Yield: a good dozen patties.
Should be consumed within a day of making or frozen.

8 oz (200 g) shoulder pork
8 oz (200 g) stewing veal
8 oz (200 g) beef suet
breadcrumbs from 4–6 slices brown bread
freshly grated rind of 1 lemon
1 level teaspoon ground sage
½ level teaspoon marjoram
1 level teaspoon salt
½ level teaspoon ground nutmeg
½ level teaspoon coarsely ground pepper
1 egg yolk
cold water to mix

Pile meats and suet into your mincer, using the coarse blade, and follow with bread to clear. Mix together all ingredients using 2 teaspoons water to start mixing. Add more if necessary. Form into patties and freeze (if not to be used immediately), four to a pack in a stack, with a piece of foil in between each, in foil dishes or freezer-wrap.

Pots of cheese

A delightful gift – several pots of different cheeses to be used as an hors d'oeuvre. Infinite variety in flavour and texture can be obtained.

Recipes made of soft cheeses keep well for 2–3 weeks, covered, in the refrigerator; recipes made with harder cheeses keep for 4–6 weeks. Allow the flavours to blend for a couple of days in the refrigerator before giving.

Combine 8 oz (200 g) grated cheese (Cheddar, Gruyère, Emmenthal or Edam, or soft cheese like cream cheese, Roquefort, Brie or Camembert) at room temperature with 2 oz (50 g) unsalted butter, also at room temperature. Soft cheese should be mashed rather than grated.

Additions:

handful finely chopped walnuts, dash of tabasco and 1 teaspoon
 Dijon mustard with a *Gruyère* or *Emmenthal* base

or

$3\frac{1}{2}$ tablespoons port or madeira and a sprinkling of cayenne
 pepper and ground mace with a *Cheddar* base

or

$1\frac{1}{2}$ tablespoons Worcester sauce and 1 level tablespoon
 crumbled crisp bacon with a *cream cheese* base

or

$3\frac{1}{2}$ tablespoons dark rum, 2 level tablespoons finely chopped
 sultanas and 1 level tablespoon chopped chutney with a *cream
 cheese* base

or

$3\frac{1}{2}$ tablespoons brandy and 1 level tablespoon finely chopped
 fresh parsley with a *Roquefort* base

or

1 level tablespoon minced fresh herbs (chives, tarragon, marjoram or basil) with a *Brie* base.

Note: clear plastic tumblers make very good containers for pots
of cheese, particularly if you are giving a selection of cheeses.

Mediterranean mélange

This is a vegetable mixture, endlessly adaptable. I like it
roughly chopped, but it is very nice processed into a smooth
paste as well. The proportions given produce a mellow, balanced
flavour, but you may want to adjust them according to your
own taste. This recipe will fill two $3\frac{1}{2}$-inch soufflé dishes or
one 5-inch one. It should be kept refrigerated until given
away.

Yield: about a pint.
Keeps for at least a week in the refrigerator.

8 oz (200 g) mushrooms (flat, field ones for preference)
8 oz (200 g) olives (preferably Greek), stoned
6 oz (150 g) onions, roughly chopped
2 cloves garlic, pressed

4–6 tablespoons olive or walnut oil – good quality oil is
    imperative to the flavour
1 level teaspoon finely grated lemon rind
freshly ground pepper
chopped parsley to decorate top of mixture

In a heavy frying pan, combine mushrooms, olives, onions,
garlic and oil. Start using 4 tablespoons oil and add more if
necessary. You want to sweat the vegetables, not colour them.
When cooked but still firm, process mixture to the texture you
prefer. Blend in lemon rind and pepper. Pack into dishes,
decorate top with chopped parsley and cover top with plastic
food wrapping.

optional additions:
Add 2 oz chopped salami/chopped water chestnuts/walnut
pieces/chopped gherkin to the basic recipe.

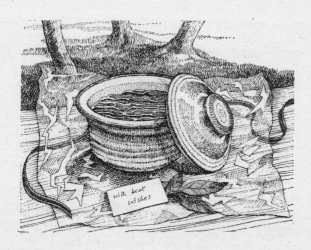

Savoury
cocktail nibbles

Giving cocktail nibbles

Cocktail biscuits and devilled nuts can be given in plastic bags, which makes carrying easy and eliminates breakage of storage jars en route to the recipient. However, they do look best in glass storage jars or family-sized instant coffee jars (give a coat of enamel paint to eradicate any lettering on the lid). The important thing is that all containers be airtight.

If you are mailing any of the produce from the recipes in this section, use a metal cake tin or plastic food storage jar, packed carefully and tightly to minimize movement, and then set the tin or jar in a cardboard box (see p. 16–17 for general notes on posting and also on labelling and storing).

Curried nuts and bolts

This is a splendid jumble of nuts and leftover plain wheat or oat cereals, very crunchy and virtually 'unputdownable'. Leftover dry cereal that is a bit stale is fine to use.

Yield: about 1 lb (400 g).
Keeps up to a month but for crispness best consumed soon after making.
Oven: preheated to 400° (mark 6).

8 oz (200 g) mixed nuts, shelled (walnuts, skinned almonds, brazils, filberts)
8 oz (200 g) bite-size shredded wheat or oat cereal (*not* flakes and *not* sugared, nor varieties that are tiny or easily shattered)
a few pretzel sticks may be included if liked

2 oz (50 g) butter   or more as required – some
2 tablespoons olive   cereals absorb more than others
oil
1 level teaspoon seasoned salt
1 level teaspoon curry powder (more if liked)
1 level teaspoon dry mustard
salt to sprinkle

Combine nuts and cereals and put into a roasting pan. Combine all other ingredients in a small saucepan and heat until mixture is bubbling. Pour over nuts and cereals and toss so each piece is well coated. Spread evenly in a single layer in a roasting pan and bake for 5–10 minutes, until the cereals are well browned. Drain on paper towels, patting to remove as much oil as possible. When completely cold, sprinkle with salt before storing.

Herb nuts and bolts: substitute for curry powder and dry mustard, 1 teaspoon each powdered sage, freeze-dried chives and tarragon and a sprinkling of garlic powder.

Salty biscuits

This is a basic recipe for biscuits to accompany cocktails and is adjustable in many ways.

Yield: about 4 dozen biscuits.
Keep well up to 2 weeks: can be frozen.
Oven: preheated to 350° (mark 4).

5 oz (125 g) self-raising flour
3 oz (75 g) butter, at room temperature
½ level teaspoon seasoned salt
1 egg for brushing, beaten
sea salt to sprinkle on top

Combine flour, butter and seasoned salt and blend into a soft, easy-to-handle ball. Pull off pieces of dough about the size of marbles and roll into round shapes. Flatten slightly. Brush lightly with egg and sprinkle with sea salt. Bake on greased baking sheets for 15–20 minutes until biscuits brown. Cool on a cooling rack before storing.

Cheese biscuits: substitute 1 oz (25 g) Parmesan cheese for 1 oz (25 g) flour and add ½ level teaspoon dry mustard.

Herb biscuits: add 2 level teaspoons dried mixed herbs to the basic recipe.

Bacon biscuits: add 2 level teaspoons crushed, well-cooked bacon to the basic recipe and omit salt.

Devilled nuts

Almost any nut will suit this recipe, but smooth-skinned ones like brazils or almonds are nicest. Buy whole, unshelled nuts, as they are cheaper than prepared ones and generally fresher.

Yield: about 1 lb (400 g).
Keep well.
Oven: preheated to 250° (mark ½).

1 lb (400 g) nuts, shelled weight
2½ tablespoons olive oil
2 level tablespoons sea salt
½ level teaspoon cayenne pepper
½ level teaspoon dry mustard

Shell nuts and remove skins, if necessary, by plunging them into boiling water and removing skins with the tip of a sharp knife. Place skinned nuts on a piece of paper towelling to dry thoroughly before tossing them in olive oil. When completely coated, lay the nuts on a baking sheet and sprinkle them with salt, cayenne and mustard powder. Bake for 1¼ hours, then turn up the heat to 350° (mark 4) for 15 minutes until the nuts are brown. Keep an eye on them so they don't burn. Allow to cool completely before storing.

Sweet sauces

Giving sauces

A very handy and most welcome present is a selection, in small jars, of sauces for ice cream or plain puddings. These can be kept in the refrigerator in screw-top jars and are instantly on hand when needed. If the sauce gets very thick upon chilling, it can be heated gently before serving.

A selection of 3 or 4 different kinds of sauce in $\frac{1}{4}$ lb jars makes a thoughtful and delicious gift (see p. 25 for suggestions on how to package these together). If you are posting sauces, bottle them in boilable plastic jars (see pp. 16–17 for general notes on posting and labelling).

All these sauces can be frozen: their high sugar content may make them go slightly syrupy, so give them a good stir before serving if they have been frozen.

Sterilization: the jars for sauces should always be sterilized. Wash jars in soap and water, rinse them out and turn upside down to drain. Put jars in a roasting pan with an inch of water in the bottom and put in a 300° (mark 2) oven for about 15 minutes, until the water is almost bubbling, the jars too hot to touch and the insides completely dry.

Milk chocolate sauce

Keeps about a month in the fridge.
Yield: 1 pint ($\frac{1}{2}$ litre).

4 oz (100 g) unsweetened cocoa powder
1 pint ($\frac{1}{2}$ litre) milk
8 oz (200 g) sugar
1 level teaspoon cornflour
$\frac{1}{2}$ oz (12 g) butter
1 teaspoon vanilla essence

Combine cocoa, milk, sugar and cornflour in a heavy saucepan over a medium heat, stirring constantly until thick and smooth. Beat in butter and vanilla and continue beating until the mixture is thick and glossy, which should be in under 5 minutes. Pour into hot sterilized jars, seal, and allow to cool completely before storing in the refrigerator.

Plain chocolate sauces

Keep about a month in the refrigerator.
Yield: 1 pint ($\frac{1}{2}$ litre).

4 oz (100 g) unsweetened cocoa powder
8 oz (200 g) sugar
4 fl oz (100 ml) golden syrup
4 fl oz (100 ml) boiling water
4 fl oz (100 ml) single cream
$1\frac{1}{2}$ oz (37 g) butter
1 teaspoon vanilla essence

Combine all ingredients except vanilla essence in a heavy saucepan and stir together over a medium heat until the sugar is dissolved and all ingredients blended. Bring to the boil and boil for about 5 minutes until sauce is thick. Remove from heat and stir in vanilla. Pour into hot, sterilized jars, seal, and allow to cool completely before storing in the refrigerator.

Variations:
Mocha: add 2 level teaspoons instant coffee powder.
Peppermint: add 1 teaspoon peppermint essence.
Orange: add $2\frac{1}{2}$ tablespoons Grand Marnier or Cointreau.
Brandy: add $2\frac{1}{2}$ tablespoons brandy.

Melba sauce

Keeps about a month in the refrigerator.
Yield: 1 pint ($\frac{1}{2}$ litre).

10 oz (250 g) raspberries (fresh or frozen)
4 fl oz (100 ml) red currant jelly
4 oz (100 g) sugar
grated rind of $\frac{1}{2}$ lemon
1 level teaspoon cornflour slaked in 1 tablespoon water

Put raspberries through a Mouli (using the fine blade) or sieve to remove seeds. Combine raspberry purée and all other ingredients in a heavy saucepan and stir over a medium heat until the mixture is thick and begins to clear. Pour into hot, sterilized jars, seal and allow to cool completely before storing in the refrigerator.

Variation: almost any berries (strawberry, red currant, black currant, blackberry) make lovely fruit sauces. Adjust sugar according to tartness of fruit, but otherwise proceed as above.

Coffee sauce

Keeps about a month in the refrigerator.
Yield: 1 pint ($\frac{1}{2}$ litre).

12 oz (300 g) soft brown sugar
8 fl oz (200 ml) water
3$\frac{1}{2}$ tablespoons golden syrup
2 oz (50 g) butter
1 oz (25 g) instant coffee powder (adjust to personal taste)

Combine all ingredients in a heavy saucepan and bring to the boil, boiling until mixture is fairly thick, about 5 minutes. Pour into hot, sterilized jars, seal and cool completely before storing in the refrigerator.

Coffee-brandy sauce: add 3$\frac{1}{2}$ tablespoons brandy when basic sauce is cool and before pouring into jars.

Butterscotch nut sauce

Keeps about a month in the refrigerator.
Yield: 1 pint ($\frac{1}{2}$ litre).

4 fl oz (100 ml) golden syrup
4 fl oz (100 ml) boiling water
4 oz (100 g) soft brown sugar
4 fl oz (100 ml) single cream
1 teaspoon vanilla essence
4 oz (100 g) chopped walnuts

Combine all ingredients except vanilla and nuts in a heavy saucepan and bring mixture to the boil. Stir constantly at the boil for 5 minutes. Allow to cool slightly before adding vanilla and nuts. Pour into hot, sterilized jars, seal, and cool completely before storing in the refrigerator.

Butterscotch rum nut sauce: add 3½ tablespoons rum when adding vanilla and nuts to cooled basic sauce.

Marron Sauce

See recipe for marrons glacés p. 99.

Apricot butter with rum

This is a marvellous substitute for brandy butter. Ideally you should pack it into small earthenware or china pots with widish tops and cover them with plastic wrap or foil, held around the top by an elastic band or ribbon. You could alternatively pack it in decorated plastic cups or foil pudding basins.

Yield: about 1 lb (400 g).
Keeps for about a month in the refrigerator.

3 oz (75 g) dried apricots, cut into eighths with scissors
8 oz (200 g) unsalted butter, softened
1 tablespoon rum
1 oz (25 g) ground almonds
finely grated rind of ½ lemon
½ teaspoon vanilla essence

Put apricots in a small bowl, just cover with water and leave to soak overnight. Drain and combine all other ingredients with the soaked apricots in a small deep bowl or blender. Blend at the lowest speed until a smooth paste is obtained or mash with a fork. Pack into small pots and refrigerate.

Sweetmeats

Giving sweetmeats

Deciding what to package sweetmeats in will depend on how many you want to give and what they look like and how sticky they are.

Sugared peel and sugared nuts are splendid candidates for glass storage jars, as they are pretty and keep their shape well. The same is true of toffee, but as it tends to go a bit sticky it is best to wrap each piece in plastic wrap or coloured cellophane before storing. Marrons glacés also need to be individually wrapped before storing. Toffee could be given cut into pieces but left unwrapped and put in a foil dish, with plastic wrap, foil or greaseproof paper between layers. It is useful to keep the brown paper cups from chocolate boxes to use for your own candy production.

Softer, denser candies like apple candy or quince sweetmeats really are best kept in airtight containers where they can lie flat and where they are less likely to lose their surface sugar. Fudge and pralines are also best stored flat, again with plastic wrap, foil or greaseproof paper between layers. Small cake tins, plastic boxes with lids designed for the refrigerator or foil dishes are fine for storing and giving these in. If you are using foil dishes, make your own cover for them with a piece of plastic wrap fastened with a big elastic band.

Toffee apples need to be wrapped individually in plastic wrap. Then sit 4, or as many as fit, in a small foil dish, with the sticks standing straight up and the apples sitting square on the bottom. Overwrap the whole thing with plastic wrap and tie with a ribbon.

See pp. 16–17 for general notes on storing and posting.

Toffee apples

Apples on a stick always mean autumn to me. I like the toffee without the addition of red food colouring, with the apples' own skin markings showing through the glaze of toffee. Save the sticks from ice creams or ice lollies to impale apples on. Be sure the sticks are well washed and dried before using.

95

Yield: 12 apples.
Don't keep well and shouldn't be made more than a day before giving.

12 hard eating apples (Cox or Granny Smiths preferred)
12 ice cream sticks
12 oz (300 g) sugar
6 fl oz (150 ml) water
1 teaspoon lemon juice

Wash apples, let dry and remove any stalk and flower centre. Impale on stick so that apple is securely held. Melt the sugar in the water over a very low heat, add lemon juice and boil rapidly without stirring until a caramel forms. Tip from side to side to produce an even caramel. Watch this carefully so the toffee doesn't burn. Turn off heat and quickly turn each apple in the toffee until it is thoroughly coated. Twirl it over the pan until the toffee begins to solidify.

Allow apples to harden by standing each apple in turn on a piece of oiled foil in a cool place. When the toffee is set and hard, cover each apple in plastic wrap and secure by twirling loose ends around the stick.

Old-fashioned toffee

Real toffee is so easy to make and so different from mass-produced. The only drawback (rapidly eliminated by its consumption) is that this toffee is a bit sticky.

Yield: about 2 lb (800 g) with nuts.
Keeps well, but do not leave in a warm place.

8 oz (200 g) butter
1 lb (400 g) dark soft brown sugar
1 tablespoon golden syrup
½ level teaspoon ground ginger
juice of 1 lemon

optional additons:
4 oz (100 g) chopped walnuts or almonds
1 teaspoon peppermint essence (omit ginger)
½ teaspoon almond essence (omit ginger)

In a heavy saucepan combine butter, sugar, golden syrup and ginger, stirring with a wooden spoon over a low heat. Gradually add lemon juice and bring mixture to the boil and allow to boil gently until the soft ball stage is reached – that is, when a drop of syrup forms a soft ball when dropped into cold water (candy thermometer 240°); this should be about 10 minutes. Add whatever optional ingredient you fancy and pour the toffee into a flat, buttered pan. Allow to cool and before it is cold cut into bite-sized pieces, dipping knife into boiling water to keep the toffee from sticking.

Apple candy

This is a kind of apple Turkish Delight, chewy and delicious. The proportions of the ingredients in this recipe are a bit inexact as the amount of sugar to add depends on your taste and the tartness of the apples.

Yield: about 1 lb (400 g).
Keeps well.

6 big cooking apples
8 oz (200 g) caster sugar
1 egg white
granulated sugar to dredge

Wash and core apples and bake until soft (about $1\frac{1}{2}$ hours in a hot oven). Remove skins, scraping off any apple that clings. Put the cooked apple through a Mouli, sieve or blender and combine with sugar. Taste, and if too tart add more sugar. The mixture should be smooth. Beat in egg white and spread mixture in a foil-lined roasting pan or 2 foil dishes. Put into plate-warming part of your cooker (or oven turned on lowest setting) for several hours. The timing will depend on how thick you spread the purée. The usual time for 1 inch depth is about 5 hours. Remove from heat, cut into squares and dredge with sugar. Allow to cool completely before packaging.

Note: to pretty up this candy, which is a nothing sort of colour, add a drop of food colouring, red or green, to the basic apple purée.

Quince sweetmeats

Fresh quinces aren't always easy to find and require effort to peel, but any energy expended is well worthwhile when the result is quince sweetmeats, a sort of quince Turkish Delight. The firm jelly is cut into squares and rolled in icing sugar, to be eaten as it is or as a dessert with cream cheese.

Yield: depends on the number of quinces you can obtain.
Keep exceptionally well up to a couple of months.

quinces, peeled and cored
water
granulated sugar
icing sugar

Put the quinces into a preserving pan and add enough water to three-quarters cover them. Cook gently until the fruit is very soft. Strain. Mash the quinces with a potato masher. Measure quince purée and add an equal quantity of sugar, combining the two in a preserving pan. Cook gently, stirring constantly, until the fruit has become amber-coloured and begins to come away from the sides of the pan. This may take quite a while, so persevere. When the purée is thick – it may have gone through a volcanic state, so don't stand too close to the pan, and use a long-handled spoon – pour into a shallow oiled baking dish, or oiled, foil-lined roasting pan, and allow to cool. When the candy has set into a firm jelly and is quite cold, cut into 1½-inch squares, roll in icing sugar and store.

Marrons glacés

These cost the earth when bought in fancy packages and are so easy to make at home in the autumn when chestnuts are harvested. If you bottle the syrup in which the chestnuts are cooked, including the pieces of chestnut that have broken off, you will have a splendid sauce for ice cream or puddings.

Yield: about 2 lb (800 g).
Keep well. Sauce keeps well for about 3 months.

3 lb (1200 g) raw chestnuts
1½ lb (600 g) sugar
1½ lb (600 g) powdered glucose (from chemist or health food
    shop)
1 pint (½ litre) water
1 vanilla bean pod

Boil raw chestnuts until they are tender and easy to peel (about 20 minutes). If they peel easily when raw, do so before boiling. Handle gently. In a heavy saucepan combine sugar, glucose and water and cook over a low heat until sugar is dissolved, then boil about 5 minutes to form a syrup. Add peeled, boiled chestnuts and vanilla pod. Boil briefly (about 2 minutes) and remove from heat, keeping pan in a warmish place. The next day, boil the chestnuts and syrup again. Again keep overnight and repeat process the next day. Remove whole chestnuts from syrup with a slotted spoon and allow to cool and drain on a cooling rack. Wrap individually and store.

Boil the remaining syrup, with bits of chestnut in it, until it thickens and bottle for marron sauce.

Food as Presents

Sugared peel

Almost any citrus fruit makes good sugared peel, but it is best to choose fruit with as thick a skin as possible. I think a mixture of peel looks prettiest.

Yield: about 1 lb (400 g).
Keeps only about a week; after that it goes soggy.

8 oz (200 g) peel (this will be about 6 oranges or 3 grapefruit
   or 8 lemons, or combination thereof)
water with a pinch of bicarbonate of soda added
1 lb (400 g) sugar

Remove the peel from the fruit and scrape off most of the pith. Cut into ½-inch wide strips, about 2 inches in length. Although more delicate strips look attractive, they tend to disintegrate in cooking. Cover peel with water, bring to the boil, drain, cover with water, bring to the boil, drain and repeat once again. Each water bath should contain a pinch of bicarbonate of soda. On the last boiling, reserve about 8 fl oz (200 ml) liquid. Remove peel. Add the sugar to the water, cook over a low heat until the sugar is dissolved, then boil about 5 minutes to form a syrup. Add peel and boil until a drop of syrup forms a soft ball when dropped into cold water (candy thermometer 240°). Remove from heat and cool, stirring occasionally until the syrup begins to thicken noticeably. Remove peel with a slotted spoon to a cooling rack. The syrup should coat each piece of peel and begin to crystallize. For a more sugary look, dust peel with granulated or caster sugar before storing.

If the peel persists in being sticky, as sometimes happens when it is very oily, you can help the drying process by placing your cooling rack in a 250° (mark ½) oven for about 30 minutes. Then cool. It is important that the peel be completely cold before storing.

Sugared nuts

Usually reserved for holiday parties, sugared nuts look pretty festive at any time.

Yield: about 1½ lb (600 g).
Keep well for weeks.
Oven: preheated to 350° (mark 4).

1 lb (400 g) mixed unsalted whole nuts (no peanuts)
1 level teaspoon salt
12 oz (300 g) light soft brown sugar
6 fl oz (150 ml) golden syrup
4 fl oz (100 ml) water
3 oz (75 g) butter
1 level teaspoon ground nutmeg
1 teaspoon vanilla essence

Combine nuts and salt and spread on a greased baking sheet and bake for about 10 minutes. Turn off oven but leave nuts in it to keep warm.

Combine sugar, golden syrup and water in a saucepan over a medium heat and stir until sugar is completely dissolved. Continue simmering, without stirring, until syrup dropped into a bowl of cold water becomes hard, but not brittle (candy thermometer 290°). Remove from heat and immediately stir in nuts, butter, nutmeg and vanilla. Quickly pour on to a greased baking sheet and spread evenly to edges. Cool completely on cooling rack. Break up nuts and store.

Variation: substitute whole almonds (blanched) for mixed nuts and almond essence for vanilla.

Cashew brittle

This is old-fashioned brittle, equally nice made with peanuts or walnuts.

Yield: about 3 lb (1¼ kg).
Keeps almost indefinitely, but shouldn't last that long!

2 lb (800 g) sugar
8 fl oz (200 ml) golden syrup
1 pint (½ litre) water
2 lb (800 g) unsalted nuts
2 level teaspoons bicarbonate of soda
1 oz (25 g) butter

Combine sugar, golden syrup and water in a saucepan over medium heat. When sugar is dissolved, increase heat and boil syrup, stirring constantly until liquid brittle forms a thin thread when dropped from the bowl of a spoon. Remove from heat and quickly stir in nuts, soda and butter. Blend thoroughly. Spread on greased swiss roll pans, distributing evenly. Allow to cool completely. Break up into pieces and store.

Infinite variety fudge

This is quite a hard fudge which can be made in an almost endless variety of flavours by additions to the basic recipe. It is a bit more work, but rather than cutting fudge into traditional squares or diamonds when hard, try putting the cooked fudge into shaped biscuit cutters. The tip of a sharp knife will help ease the hardened fudge out of the moulds, and you will have a pleasing array of shapes to your fudge. As all the varieties of fudge listed start with the basic recipe, you can make several types of fudge at a time by dividing the cooked fudge into 2 or 3 lots, adding a different flavour to each.

Yield: about 1 lb (400 g).
Keeps well if carefully stored.

5 tablespoons milk
5 tablespoons single cream
10 oz (250 g) granulated sugar
8 oz (200 g) light, soft brown sugar
½ oz (12 g) butter
½ level teaspoon cream of tartar
flavouring as below

Combine milk and cream in a heavy saucepan and bring just to the boil. Remove from heat and add all other ingredients except flavouring. Stir constantly over a low heat until the sugar has melted but do not boil. Uncover and allow to boil gently until the soft ball stage – that is when a soft ball is formed when a bit of fudge is dropped into cold water (candy thermometer 240°). Remove from heat and beat fudge with a wooden spoon until it thickens. Add flavouring, mix well and pour into 12 greased moulds or a 9-inch square baking tin, lined with greased foil to facilitate removal of fudge. Allow to harden before turning out, cutting and storing.

Flavours:

Chocolate: add 2 level tablespoons unsweetened cocoa powder to basic recipe.

Coffee: add 1 level tablespoon instant coffee powder to basic recipe.

Vanilla: add 1 tablespoon vanilla essence to basic recipe.

Ginger: add 1 level teaspoon ground ginger and 1 oz (25 g) chopped candied ginger to basic recipe.

Almond: add 2 teaspoons almond essence to basic recipe and press a whole blanched almond into top of each piece of fudge.

Lemon: add 2 teaspoons lemon essence to basic recipe and press a bit of candied peel into top of each piece of fudge.

Chocolate/Peppermint: add 2 teaspoons peppermint essence to basic recipe and dot top of cooling fudge with chocolate bits.

Pralines

Pralines are a delectable confection, combining the flavours of brown sugar and nuts. They originated in the southern part of America, where pecans abound; however, walnut halves will substitute if you cannot find unsalted pecans. They are delicate in both taste and handling.

Yield: about a dozen 2-inch patties.
Will keep up to a month, if carefully stored in a cool place.

8 oz (200 g) sugar
4 oz (100 g) light soft brown sugar
4 fl oz (100 ml) single cream
12 oz (200 g) pecan halves
1 oz (25 g) butter

Combine sugars and cream in a heavy saucepan and, stirring constantly, cook over a low heat until the sugar has dissolved. Then boil until the syrup spins a thread when dropped from the spoon. Remove from heat and add nuts and butter. Stir well. Return to the heat and continue stirring until the soft ball stage is reached – that is, when a drop of syrup forms a soft ball when dropped into cold water (candy thermometer 240°). Remove from heat and allow to rest for 10–15 minutes, by which time the mixture will be quite thick and glossy.

Drop pralines, about 6 to each baking sheet, by rounded tablespoonfuls onto a greased baking sheet. They will spread out to a diameter of about 2 inches. If the mixture seems very thick, you can add cold water, a drop at a time, to loosen it somewhat. Allow pralines to set and become quite cold before storing carefully.

Booze bombs

This is a splendid (some say preferable) alternative to chocolate truffles. They should be made several days before giving, stored in plastic bags in the refrigerator, so that the flavours blend and mellow.

Yield: about 48 balls, 1 inch in diameter.
Keep well in covered container or plastic bags, preferably in refrigerator.

8 oz (200 g) chocolate chips, melted
4 fl oz (100 ml) golden syrup
3 fl oz (75 ml) brandy
4 fl oz (100 ml) whisky or dark rum
1 lb (400 g) plain biscuits (Rich Tea preferred) crushed fine
1 8 oz (200 g) package mixed chopped nuts, processed until
   finely chopped but not ground
icing sugar for dredging

Combine all ingredients except icing sugar and blend well. Roll rounded tablespoonfuls of mixture in your hands to form balls. Roll balls in icing sugar. Place on trays in refrigerator until hardened and then pack into covered containers or plastic bags. Keep in refrigerator until giving.

Baked goods

Giving baked goods

For the most part, baked things other than breads are best packed and given in airtight containers, such as cake tins or plastic refrigerator boxes, which will protect their crispness or moistness and keep them from getting bashed around. Biscuits, especially those made by dropping dough by the spoonful on a baking sheet, are generally pretty sturdy and will probably be fine packed in plastic bags, securely tied. The same is true for bread or muffins, and these are a particularly good idea if the person to whom you are giving them has a freezer in which to store baked goods for future use. (Under the heading 'Biscuits' I have given recipes for 'Cookies'; the former term is English, the latter American, for in America a biscuit is more like an English scone – a confusing situation!)

Plastic food bags keep baked things from drying out, which is why they are useful, but there is one drawback. A moist cake or loaf of bread in a plastic bag left for several days in a warm room may spell mould. If you are baking a week or so before giving, keep moist baked goods in plastic bags in the refrigerator. The important thing to remember is that whatever container you use should be airtight.

I tend to think that whatever I bake for giving is going to be used immediately, which isn't always true. Some of the best presents are those you can turn to in an emergency (bless the freezer) or eat when the gorging of holidays is past. Of course many baked things don't last longer than the announcement that they exist, but it is food for thought to think in terms of giving people with freezers baked goods for future use, rather than immediate consumption. Almost all baked goods freeze well.

Whatever baked goods you give should be super-fresh, and if they need special instructions (if they should be eaten right away, heated up, keep well, etc.), be sure to tell the recipient.

I haven't included recipes which heavily feature icing or gooey fillings because they are not reliable when entrusted to the posts or subjected to changing climatic conditions. If you are giving baked goods in person, rather than posting them, naturally your choice of what to give will be infinitely wider.

See p. 16 for general notes on labelling and storing.

Posting baked goods

Think of your home-produced baked goods as exceedingly fragile, whether or not they are, when considering posting them as gifts. If they are to survive the possible rigours of the postal system, they will have to be protected and securely packed so that they arrive in the same state as they left your kitchen. Common sense above all should prevail when deciding what to send, bearing in mind how far it has to travel, the toll the present weather conditions will take, etc. Obviously, heat and damp will cause baked goods, even when packed in airtight conditions, to deteriorate faster than when they are sent in the dead of winter.

Posting bread: bake the bread in disposable foil loaf tins. Leave the completely cooled bread in the tins and insert the bread and tin into a plastic food wrap bag, secured with the tie-band supplied with the bag. *The bread must be completely cold.* Now pack into a sturdy cardboard box (see p. 17).

If you cannot find disposable foil tins, bake in your usual loaf tin and cool the bread. Using the large size (35 fl oz) juice tin, washed and dried, remove one end completely. Put the bread in a plastic food wrap bag and insert into tin. Surround the bread with wadded up paper towels, napkins or the bags that dry cleaning is returned in; the idea again is that no movement be possible within the tin. Then proceed with the boxing, etc.

Posting cookies and biscuits: choose only sturdy cookies to post, as there is little point in sending what will only arrive as a mass of crumbs. If you are sending a selection, pack with the heaviest at the bottom. Wrap each cookie, or sometimes two together, in food wrap and pack them in empty tins, refrigerator boxes etc., anything to protect them, and then into cardboard boxes as above.

Posting cakes: pack loaf cakes as for bread, though it is better to make the lemon cake without glaze if posting. The ring cakes could be packed, with great ingenuity, but I wouldn't really advise you to try.

Biscuits

Peanut butter cookies

Children particularly like these very crisp biscuits. They can be made in quantity without having to wash up baking sheets in between batches, by using greased sheets of aluminium foil and dropping dough onto them in advance. As one batch finishes baking, its cookies go onto the cooling rack and the new batch slides onto the baking sheet and into the oven without delay. As for the baking sheets, borrow or buy a couple of extra ones – 4 sheets ought to suffice for mass production and allow time for them to cool between batches.

Yield: about 6 dozen.
Keep very well.
Oven: preheated to 400° (mark 6).

8 oz (200 g) soft butter
8 oz (200 g) sugar
8 oz (200 g) dark soft brown sugar
2 eggs
1 teaspoon vanilla essence
12 oz (300 g) plain flour
1 level teaspoon salt
1½ level teaspoons bicarbonate of soda
8 oz (200 g) crunchy peanut butter

Cream butter and sugars together until smooth. Beat in eggs and vanilla essence. Sift together flour, salt and soda and fold in to butter mixture. When smooth fold in peanut butter, blending well. Roll balls of dough – a scant tablespoonful per cookie – between your palms and place about an inch apart on a greased baking sheet or greased aluminium foil as suggested above. Flatten each cookie with the tines of a fork, dipped in sugar, making a crisscross pattern on the top. Bake for about 8 minutes or until cookies are browned at the edges. Cool on cooling rack before storing.

For a frosted look to the cookies, dust with sugar before baking after you've made the crisscross design on the top.

Fruit and nut clusters

These are great to make in quantity (see previous recipe), and a good choice to give to friends who have children who eat everything in sight.

Yield: about 10 dozen.
Keep very well.
Oven: preheated to 325° (mark 3).

8 oz (200 g) mixed dried fruit, diced
1 lb (400 g) seedless raisins or sultanas
3½ tablespoons sherry or rum
3½ tablespoons whisky
2 oz (50 g) soft butter
4 oz (100 g) dark soft brown sugar
2 eggs
6 oz (150 g) plain flour
1½ level tablespoons bicarbonate of soda
2 level teaspoons ground cinnamon
½ level teaspoon ground nutmeg
½ level teaspoon ground allspice
1 lb (400 g) shelled nuts in pieces (no peanuts)
8 oz (200 g) candied citrus peel diced
8 oz (200 g) glacé cherries

Soak dried fruit and raisins in liquors overnight, covered, in refrigerator. Beat together butter, sugar and eggs until light and fluffy. In a separate bowl sift together flour, soda and spices, and then combine all ingredients mixing well. Drop rounded teaspoonfuls on greased baking sheets and bake about 15 minutes. Cool on cooling rack and store when cold.

Chocolate chip cookies

This is the best recipe I've devised for them because the cookie part is a bit chewy with a splendid caramel flavour. These can be made in quantity (see recipe for peanut butter cookies).

Yield: about 3 dozen.
Keep well.
Oven: preheated to 375° (mark 5).

8 oz (200 g) soft butter
2 eggs
2 teaspoons vanilla essence
1 teaspoon water
scant 1¼ lb (500 g) plain flour
1 level teaspoon salt
1 level teaspoon bicarbonate of soda
8 oz (200 g) dark soft brown sugar
4 oz (100 g) sugar
12 oz (300 g) chocolate chips
8 oz (200 g) chopped walnuts (optional)

Cream together butter, eggs and vanilla essence. Add water and
set aside. In a separate bowl, sift together flour, salt and bicarbonate of soda. Add both sugars to the butter mixture and mix
well until blended and smooth. Fold together butter and flour
mixtures until completely amalgamated. Add chocolate chips
(and walnuts if desired) and distribute evenly throughout
mixture. Drop rounded teaspoonfuls onto greased baking
sheets leaving 2 inches between cookies. Bake about 10–12
minutes until the edges brown. Cool on a cooling rack before
storing.

The richest brownies known to man

Brownies are a typically American confection. Mid-way between cookies and cake, they are incredibly rich and deep in
flavour. Ideally, you should use unsweetened baking chocolate
such as the brand called 'Baker's chocolate' which is obtainable
at speciality grocers. Failing this, you can substitute 3 level
tablespoons unsweetened cocoa powder and ½ oz (12 g) butter
or margarine for each ounce of baking chocolate called for in
the recipe.

Yield: about 2 dozen.
Keep very well up to 2 weeks, though they begin to dry out at

the edges after a few days. As they are very rich and gooey, I suggest wrapping each in plastic wrap before storing.
Oven: preheated to 350° (mark 4).

4 eggs
8 oz (200 g) soft butter
2 teaspoons vanilla essence
6 squares (6 oz (150 g)) unsweetened baking chocolate, melted and cooled to room temperature
10 oz (250 g) plain flour
$\frac{1}{4}$ level teaspoon baking powder
$\frac{1}{2}$ level teaspoon salt
1 lb (400 g) sugar

optional additions:
6 oz (150 g) chocolate chips and/or 4 oz (100 g) chopped walnuts.

In a bowl combine eggs, butter and vanilla essence and beat with an electric mixer at the highest speed until the mixture is very light and fluffy. Beat with a wooden spoon if you haven't a mixer. Reduce speed to medium and slowly add the chocolate. Continue beating for 1 minute (or 3 minutes if beating by hand). Sift together flour, baking powder, salt and sugar and then fold into chocolate mixture, blending completely. Fold in chocolate chips and/or walnuts if desired. Turn dough into 2 greased and floured baking tins, about 7 inches square, spreading evenly. Bake for about 40 minutes until the sides of the brownies begin to shrink away from the sides of the tin and a knife inserted in the centre comes out clean. Cool tins on a cooling rack before cutting brownies into squares and storing.

Chocolate snowcaps

These are fudgy, soft cookies with a crisp sugar crust. They are a bit fragile.

Yield: about 5 dozen.
Keep moderately well, but lose some of their crisp crust after 2–3 days.
Oven: preheated to 350° (mark 4).

4 oz (100 g) unsweetened cocoa powder
6 fl oz (150 ml) vegetable oil (not peanut or olive)
1 lb (400 g) sugar
2 teaspoons vanilla essence
4 eggs
12½ oz (312 g) plain flour
½ level teaspoon salt
2 level teaspoons baking powder
icing sugar to dredge

Beat together until smooth cocoa, oil, sugar, vanilla and eggs. Sift together flour, salt and baking powder and fold into chocolate mixture. Blend well and chill overnight in a covered bowl. Mould rounded teaspoonfuls of dough between palms and roll in icing sugar until thoroughly coated. Space cookies at least 1½ inches apart on baking sheets and bake about 12 minutes, until the surface is crinkled and crisp, while the inside is still soft. Cool completely on a cooling rack before storing with care.

Coconut macaroons

These are wonderfully chewy but still very light.

Yield: about 2 dozen.
Keep badly as they dry out quickly: should be made and eaten within 2 days. Cannot be frozen.
Oven: preheated to 300° (mark 2).

3 large egg whites
8 oz (200 g) sugar
1 oz (25 g) cornflour
5 oz (125 g) moist shredded coconut
1 teaspoon vanilla essence
1 teaspoon almond essence

Beat egg whites until stiff but not dry. Continue beating, adding sugar a little at a time. Mix the cornflour with the coconut and fold into the egg white mixture. Cook mixture on top of a bain marie over simmering water for about 15 minutes, stirring constantly. Remove pan from heat and stir in vanilla and almond essences. Drop tablespoonfuls onto greased baking sheets, leaving 1½ inches between each macaroon. Bake for about 25 minutes until delicately browned. Cool on a cooling rack before storing.

Italian dry macaroons

These are the small, dry macaroons one finds in the best Italian restaurants. They are light as air and have a distinctive almond flavour.

Yield: about 2 dozen.
Keep extremely well.
Oven: preheated to 350° (mark 4).

4 oz (100 g) ground almonds
6 oz (150 g) caster sugar
2 large egg whites (or 3 standard ones)
1½ tablespoons Kirsch
½ teaspoon vanilla essence
icing sugar for dredging

With pestle and mortar pound together almonds and caster sugar with half the egg white. Beat the remaining egg white until very stiff and fold it, together with the Kirsch and vanilla essence into the almond mixture. Gently and quickly roll rounded teaspoonfuls of dough between your palms and place balls on non-stick paper on a baking sheet. Bake for about 30 minutes until macaroons are puffed and a bit cracked. Dredge with icing sugar and cool completely on a cooling rack before storing.

Pfeffernuesse

These are the small cake-like cookies that are covered in icing sugar that appear in speciality bakers around Christmas time. They taste of cinnamon and citron.

Yield: about 5 dozen.
Keep very well – up to a month.
Oven: preheated to 350° (mark 4).

6 fl oz (150 ml) cold strong black coffee
2 oz (50 g) sugar
13 tablespoons molasses
4 oz (100 g) soft butter
juice and rind of 1 lemon
4 oz (100 g) dark soft brown sugar
1¼ lb (500 g) plain flour
1 level teaspoon bicarbonate of soda
1 level teaspoon ground cinnamon
1 level teaspoon ground ginger
1 level teaspoon ground cloves
2 oz (50 g) chopped candied citrus peel
2 oz (50 g) ground almonds
1 egg white, for brushing, lightly beaten
icing sugar to dredge

Beat together until blended, coffee, sugar, molasses, butter, lemon juice and rind and brown sugar. Sift together the flour, soda and spices and fold into the liquid mixture. When thoroughly blended, fold in citrus peel and ground almonds. Roll small (about a teaspoonful) balls of dough between your palms and set out quite close together on greased baking sheets. Brush with egg white and bake for about 10 minutes, or until browned. Cool partially on cooling rack and while still warm roll them in icing sugar, allowing pfeffernuesse to cool before storing.

Shortbread

Traditionally, shortbread was the Scottish wedding cake, and a piece put under the pillow, it was said, would make a maiden lady dream of the man she would marry.

Shortbread is best made of a combination of plain and rice flours, the latter giving it a splendid texture and crunch: however, if rice flour or ground rice isn't available use the full flour complement in plain flour.

Yield: about a dozen pieces.
Keeps very well.
Oven: preheated to 325° (mark 3).

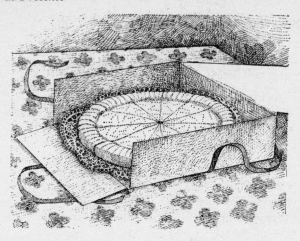

5 oz (125 g) plain flour, sifted
1 oz (25 g) rice flour or ground rice
3 oz (75 g) soft butter
2 oz (50 g) sugar
sugar to dredge

Rub flours and butter together until the mixture is crumbly.
Blend in sugar and knead together to blend well. Pat into greased
7–8 inch baking tin fairly firmly. Prick all over with the tines of
a fork. Bake for about 45 minutes. Cut into squares or triangles
while in the baking tin and still hot and allow to cool completely in the tin on a cooling rack. Dredge with sugar before
storing.

Variation: for a glazed top, brush top of unbaked shortbread
with unbeaten egg white, taking care not to disturb dough and
sprinkle with slivered almonds and sugar.

Ginger shortbread: add 1 oz (25 g) ground ginger to flours and
proceed as in above recipe.

Swedish sugar cookies

These are crunchy cookies, tasting wonderfully of butter, cinnamon and vanilla. They are easily made (perfect if kids want to help) and travel well.

Yield: about 2½ dozen.
Keep very well. They are sturdy cookies and can well be given in quantity in plastic bags.
Oven: preheated to 400° (mark 6).

8 oz (200 g) very soft butter
6 oz (150 g) sugar
1 teaspoon vanilla essence
14 oz (350 g) plain flour
1 level teaspoon baking powder
equal parts ground cinnamon and sugar to dredge

Cream together until light and fluffy butter, sugar and vanilla essence. Sift together flour and baking powder and fold into butter mixture. Make balls about 1 inch in diameter by rolling dough between your palms and then roll balls in the cinnamon-sugar mixture. Bake on greased baking sheets for about 10 minutes until they begin to brown and the surface is cracked. Cool on cooling rack before storing.

Yorkshire parkins

These are chewy cookies somewhere between oatmeal cookies and gingersnaps.

Yield: about 3 dozen.
Keep very well; travel well.
Oven: preheated to 350° (mark 4).

1 level teaspoon bicarbonate of soda
12 oz (300 g) quick-cooking oatmeal
4 oz (100 g) plain flour
1 level teaspoon ground ginger
1 level teaspoon ground cinnamon
1 level teaspoon ground nutmeg
4 fl oz (100 ml) molasses

4 fl oz (100 ml) golden syrup
4 oz (100 g) soft butter
3½ tablespoons milk
finely grated rind of 1 lemon

Mix together until completely blended the soda, oatmeal, flour
and spices and set aside. Beat together the molasses, golden
syrup, butter, milk and lemon rind. Fold in dry mixture and
blend thoroughly. Pour mixture evenly into greased baking tins
(at least 1 inch deep) or roasting pans, smoothing to the edges,
and bake for about 1¼ hours until browned. The mixture
should be about ½-inch thick. Cool on cooling rack and cut
into squares when still warm, allowing to become cold before
storing.

Digestive biscuits

Homemade digestive biscuits are quite different from the mass-
produced variety readily available and are lovely on their own,
buttered or with soft cheeses.

Yield: about 2½ dozen.
Keep well.
Oven: preheated to 350° (mark 4).

3 oz (75 g) soft butter
2 oz (50 g) soft lard
3 tablespoons boiling water
1 egg
4 oz (100 g) plain flour
8 oz (200 g) wholemeal flour
½ level teaspoon salt
¼ level teaspoon ground nutmeg
2 oz (50 g) sugar

Combine butter and lard in mixing bowl, add boiling water and
beat with an electric mixer or wooden spoon until the mixture is
soft and fluffy. Beat in egg. In a separate bowl, mix together the
dry ingredients and then fold the dry ingredients into the fat
mixture, mixing just until dough cleans the bowl. Roll out on a
floured board to about ⅛-inch thickness. Prick all over with

the tines of a fork and then, using a round cutter, cut into individual biscuits 2½ inches in diameter. Bake on greased baking sheets for 25 minutes until the biscuits begin to brown at the edges. Cool on a cooling rack and store when completely cold.

Scottish oatcakes

The rough texture of oatcakes makes a splendid contrast with soft cheeses and the oaty flavour brings out almost any cheese.

Yield: about a dozen.
Keep very well, but are quite fragile.
Oven: preheated to 350° (mark 4).

10 oz (250 g) medium oatmeal
½ level teaspoon salt
3 tablespoons melted bacon fat
4 fl oz (100 ml) hot water – you may need less

Combine oatmeal and salt, then add bacon fat and enough hot water to yield a stiff dough. Roll out the dough on a floured breadboard deftly and quickly, to about ¼-inch thickness. Time is important here. Cut oatcake dough with a round cutter and transfer cakes (you may need to use a spatula to help) to a greased baking sheet. Bake for about 10 minutes, by which time the edges should just have begun to brown and slightly turn up. Cool completely on a cooling rack before storing.

Breads and muffins
Gingerbread

This recipe makes a very black gingerbread ('definitely an adult taste', says a friend) and is best made in a loaf tin, rather than a baking tin designed to produce gingerbread to be cut into squares.

Yield: 1 loaf.
Keeps splendidly at least 2 weeks.
Oven: preheated to 350° (mark 4).

5 oz (125 g) plain flour
1 level teaspoon bicarbonate of soda
1 level teaspoon ground cinnamon
½ level teaspoon ground ginger
½ level teaspoon ground cloves
½ level teaspoon ground nutmeg
½ level teaspoon ground allspice
¼ level teaspoon salt
2 oz (50 g) sugar
4 fl oz (100 ml) molasses (the crudest, blackest possible)
2 eggs
3½ oz (87 g) butter, melted
4 fl oz (100 ml) hot water
8 oz (200 g) seedless raisins or sultanas, plumped in cider and
   drained
granulated sugar to dredge

Sift together the flour, soda, spices, salt and sugar and set aside.
Beat together the molasses, egg, melted butter and hot water
until smooth and fold into the flour mixture. When completely
blended, fold in raisins and pour mixture into a greased 1 lb loaf
tin. Bake for about 45 minutes until risen and the gingerbread
begins to pull away from the sides of the tin. Cool in tin on a
cooling rack and then turn out. Dredge with sugar before storing.

A nutty loaf

This is a not-too-sweet tea bread with a full, nutty flavour. If
you plan to freeze it, do so without glazing and apply the glaze
when the loaf has thawed.

Yield: 1 loaf.
Keeps well.
Oven: preheated to 325° (mark 3).

6 oz (150 g) soft butter
3 oz (75 g) sugar
3 large eggs
4 oz (100 g) wholemeal flour
4 oz (100 g) white flour
1 tablespoon baking powder

1 oz (25 g) ground almonds
3 oz (75 g) chopped nuts, not peanuts
2 tablespoons sherry

Cream together butter, sugar and eggs. Add all other ingredients
and mix well. Pour into a greased 1 lb loaf tin, smoothing the
batter. Bake for about 1¼ hours or until the bread has risen
well and the top is browned and cracked. Leave in tin for 5
minutes before turning out to cool completely on a cooling rack.

Glaze

3 tablespoons red currant jelly or apricot jam
1 tablespoon sherry
Walnut halves/Brazil nuts/Almonds to decorate

Warm together the jelly and sherry, blending until smooth.
Brush over cool, dry cake. If you have frozen the cake after
baking and are decorating it defrosted, be sure to pat any surface
moisture away with a piece of kitchen paper.

Stick the nuts in whatever pattern you fancy on the top of the
glazed cake and then apply the glaze over the nuts as well. Cool
completely.

Banana bread

This bread, which is like gingerbread in texture, has a flavour
that is mellow and full.

Yield: 1 loaf.
Keeps well.
Oven: preheated to 350° (mark 4).

6 oz (150 g) self-raising flour
¼ level teaspoon bicarbonate of soda
½ level teaspoon salt
1½ oz (37 g) soft butter
6 oz (150 g) light soft brown sugar
2 large eggs, beaten
1 teaspoon vanilla essence
1 lb (400 g) bananas, mashed
4 oz (100 g) walnuts, chopped

Sift together flour, soda and salt and set aside. Cream together butter, sugar and eggs until light and fluffy; add vanilla essence, bananas and walnuts (reserving 1 oz (25 g) to sprinkle on top of loaf). Blend thoroughly and fold in flour mixture. Pour into a greased 1 lb loaf tin. Sprinkle reserved walnuts on top. Bake for about 1 hour until bread has risen and the top browned and a toothpick inserted in the centre comes out clean. Cool in tin for 5 minutes before turning out on to a cooling rack. Cool completely before storing.

Apple and cheese tea bread

The texture of this bread is somewhere between a bread and a cake. Lovely toasted, or warmed with jam for breakfast, or sliced and spread with butter for tea.

Yield: 1 loaf.
Keeps well.
Oven: preheated to 350° (mark 4).

4 oz (100 g) very soft butter
4 oz (100 g) sugar
2 eggs
10 oz (250 g) plain flour, sifted
1 level teaspoon baking powder
$\frac{1}{2}$ level teaspoon bicarbonate of soda
1 level teaspoon salt
1 lb (400 g) cooking apples, peeled, cored and grated
3 oz (75 g) Cheddar cheese, grated
3 oz (75 g) walnuts or pecans, chopped

Beat together butter, sugar and eggs until very light and fluffy. Sift dry ingredients together and fold into butter mixture. Mix in apples, cheese and nuts, blending quickly and completely. Turn into a greased 1 lb loaf tin and bake in the centre of the oven for about 1 hour, perhaps a bit less, until the loaf is well risen, the top browned, and a toothpick inserted in the centre comes out clean. Rest in tin for 5 minutes before turning out to complete cooling on a cooling rack.

Sarah Taylor's molasses and oatmeal bread

This a rough-textured bread, a bit crumbly and with a marvellous taste. The oatmeal called for can be found in health food shops and many grocery stores; do not use rolled oats. Serve with plenty of butter or soft cheese.

Yield: 3 loaves.
Keeps 4–5 days before it begins to get a bit dry. Freezes well.
Oven: preheated to 425° (mark 7).

7 oz (175 g) coarse or medium oatmeal
1¼ pints (625 ml) water, hand hot
8 fl oz (200 ml) molasses
1 level teaspoon salt
1 oz (25 g) dry yeast (or 2 oz fresh yeast)
1 level teaspoon sugar
2 lb (800 g) wholemeal flour
flour to knead with

Combine the oatmeal, 1 pint of water, molasses and salt in a large bowl and set aside for 10 minutes. In a separate small bowl, add the remaining water, dry yeast and sugar, stir through and allow the yeast to proof. When the surface of the yeast mixture is bubbly, pour into the large bowl containing the oatmeal, then stir in the wholemeal flour. Mix together thoroughly. Cover the bowl with a clean towel and allow the dough to rise. Hopefully the kitchen will be warm, as you want to keep the rising dough in a warm place and out of draughts. If the kitchen isn't warm, I suggest placing the bowl with the rising dough over a saucepan of hot water. Allow dough to rise for at least 1 hour and preferably 1½ hours. Remove to a well floured bread board and knead for about 10 minutes, using more flour as required. This dough is sticky and heavy so you will use quite a bit of additional flour at this point in order to achieve a smooth dough. Divide the dough into three parts and shape these into loaves, inserting them into three well greased loaf pans. Cover these with a kitchen towel, and allow the dough to rise to double its size in warm surroundings. This should take another hour or so. When the loaves have risen nicely, pop the pans into a hot oven and bake for 15–20 minutes before reducing the temperature to 400° (mark 6). Baking should take 50–60 minutes. The bread will be ready when it is well browned and sounds hollow when the bottom of the pan is tapped. Remove the loaves from their tins; if the bottom is sticky, put the loaves directly back into the oven (which you have turned off) for a few minutes to dry out a bit before removing them finally to cool thoroughly on a cooling rack.

Boston brown bread

Traditionally Boston brown bread was made in round loaves, about 6 inches in diameter and 8 inches long. The original recipe calls for a combination of wheat and rye flours with cornmeal and the dough then steamed rather than baked. This combination yields a denser, soggier bread than the recipe below, but I prefer the chewier version, and crust given. Instead of an ordinary loaf tin, I use an empty fruit juice tin (up to a 35 fl oz size) having completely removed one end, as I like the traditional shape for Boston brown bread. Coffee tins, the 1 lb size, will also serve the purpose well. This bread should be served thinly sliced and buttered.

Yield: 1 loaf.
Keeps well.
Oven: preheated to 350° (mark 4).

8 fl oz (200 ml) buttermilk (or 8 oz milk and 1 tablespoon lemon juice)
3½ tablespoons molasses
5 oz (125 g) plain flour
½ level teaspoon salt
1 level teaspoon bicarbonate of soda
1 egg
4 oz (100 g) sultanas

Mix buttermilk and molasses together. Sift together dry ingredients, and add molasses mixture to them with the egg. Blend thoroughly. Stir in sultanas. Allow dough to rest for ½ an hour before pouring into a greased container. Bake for about 45 minutes or until a toothpick inserted in the centre comes out clean. Remove the loaf carefully from pan and cool on a cooling rack. Cool completely before storing.

Marmalade muffins

These are American-type muffins, which closely resemble English cup cakes. Make them with coarse-cut marmalade, snipping the larger bits of peel with scissors before adding to dough.

Yield: a dozen muffins.
Keep very well.
Oven: preheated to 400° (mark 6).

4 oz (100 g) sugar
2 eggs beaten
8 fl oz (200 ml) milk
8 oz (200 g) plain flour
1½ level tablespoons baking powder
½ level teaspoon salt
½ level teaspoon ground allspice
½ level teaspoon ground nutmeg
2 tablespoons marmalade

Combine until blended sugar, eggs and milk. Sift together flour, baking powder, salt and spices and add to egg mixture until completely blended. Stir in marmalade. Fill greased patty tins between half and three-quarters full and bake for about 20 minutes, until muffins are raised and their tops browned. Turn out onto cooling rack and store when cold.

Apple and cinnamon muffins

The flavour of apple and cinnamon together has always been a favourite of mine. These muffins are best warmed before serving.

Yield: a dozen muffins.
Keep well.
Oven: preheated to 400° (mark 6).

1 egg, beaten
4 fl oz (100 ml) milk
a good 1½ oz butter, melted
8 oz (200 g) cooking apples, cored, peeled and chopped
6 oz (150 g) self-raising flour
½ level teaspoon salt
4 oz (100 g) sugar
1 level teaspoon ground cinnamon
dash of ground cloves
sugar to dredge

Mix together egg, milk, melted butter and apples. Sift together flour, salt, sugar and spices. Combine and blend completely. Fill greased patty tins between half and three-quarters full and bake for 20 minutes until muffins are raised and the tops browned. Turn out and dredge with sugar. Allow to cool completely before storing.

Bran muffins

There is something warm and friendly about the smell of bran muffins baking. They are lovely for breakfast just out of the oven, or toasted for tea. A nice gift for someone who has a freezer, given by the plastic bag-full.

Yield: a dozen muffins.
Keep well.
Oven: preheated to 400° (mark 6).

8 oz (200 g) all-bran cereal
12 oz (300 ml) milk
4 fl oz (100 ml) molasses
1 egg, lightly beaten
4 oz (100 g) plain flour, sifted
½ level teaspoon salt
1 level teaspoon bicarbonate of soda
2 oz (50 g) sultanas

Combine bran, milk and molasses in a bowl and allow to soak for about 20 minutes. Beat in egg. Sift flour, salt and soda, add to bran mixture and blend well. Add sultanas. Fill cups of greased patty tins between half and three-quarters full and bake for about 20 minutes, until muffins are raised and browned. Turn out and allow to cool completely before storing.

Cakes

Orange fruit cake

A nice alternative to traditional fruit cake, which combines oranges, raisins and brandy. The flavour of this cake improves on keeping, and it is best made a week or so before giving.

Yield: 1 loaf.
Keeps very well in the refrigerator up to a month.
Oven: preheated to 325° (mark 3).

juice and rind of 2 oranges
1½ lb (600 g) seedless raisins or sultanas
7 tablespoons brandy
8 oz (200 g) soft butter
8 oz (200 g) sugar
4 eggs
4 oz (100 g) plain flour
1 oz (25 g) self-raising flour
1 level teaspoon ground mace
whisky or sherry to soak cheesecloth

Combine orange rind and juice, raisins and brandy in a bowl, cover and leave overnight in refrigerator. If liquid doesn't cover raisins, stir occasionally. Cream together butter and sugar and add eggs one at a time. Beat after each addition until mixture is fluffy. Fold in flour and blend completely, but do not stir more than necessary. Add raisin mixture. Turn into greased 1 lb loaf tin and bake for about 3 hours. Cool in tin for 10 minutes until cake comes out easily. Cool cake on cooling rack until cold. Wrap in whisky or sherry-soaked cheesecloth, overwrap in foil and store in refrigerator.

Mocha dot ring cake

This is a Madeira-type cake, made in a ring mould. The chocolate chips are swirled in with half the cake mixture and the coffee flavour with the other half, giving a marbled look to the finished cake.

Yield: 1 cake.
Keeps 2–3 days in best condition.
Oven: preheated to 350° (mark 4).

8 oz (200 g) soft butter
8 oz (200 g) sugar
4 eggs
8 oz (200 g) self-raising flour
1 level tablespoon instant coffee powder, dissolved in 1
    tablespoon boiling water
6 oz (150 g) chocolate chips
sugar to dredge

Combine butter and sugar and add eggs one at a time, beating after each addition. Blend in flour. Divide mixture in half, adding dissolved instant coffee to one half, chocolate chips to the other. Cut one mixture into the other to make a marbled look – do not overdo this. Pour into a greased 3½-pint ring mould and bake for about 45 minutes until the cake is risen and the top firm. Cool for 5 minutes before turning out to finish cooling on a cooling rack. Dredge with sugar before storing.

Chocolate Madeira ring

A chocolaty plain cake that lends itself to dressing up either with a glaze or with chocolate chips in the mixture.

Yield: 1 cake.
Keeps very well without a glaze, and 3–4 days with one.
Oven: preheated to 325° (mark 3).

12 oz (300 g) soft butter
1½ lb (600 g) sugar
5 eggs
12 oz (300 g) plain flour
4 oz (100 g) unsweetened cocoa powder
½ level teaspoon baking powder
½ level teaspoon salt
½ pint (¼ litre) milk
2 teaspoons vanilla essence
6 oz (150 g) chocolate chips (optional)

Glaze
1 level tablespoon granulated sugar
1 tablespoon water
4 oz (100 g) chocolate chips

Beat together butter and sugar until light and fluffy and add eggs, one at a time. Sift all dry ingredients together and add to butter mixture alternately with milk and vanilla. Add chocolate chips, if using them. Pour into a greased 3½-pint ring mould and bake for about 1½ hours, until the cake is risen and the top firm. Let the cake rest in the tin on a cooling rack for 5 minutes before turning out to finish cooling. Glaze or dredge with sugar before storing.

To glaze, dissolve the sugar in the water over a low heat then add chocolate chips and stir until smooth. Cool slightly and pour glaze over cake when quite thick.

Glazed almond and orange cake

This is a rich cake, fragrant with orange liqueur, orange rind and almonds.

Yield: 1 cake.
Keeps well, 2–3 days.
Oven: preheated to 350° (mark 4).

8 oz (200 g) soft butter
8 oz (200 g) sugar
3 eggs, separated, with whites beaten until stiff but not dry
13 tablespoons sour cream
grated rind of 2 oranges
8 oz (200 g) plain flour
1 level teaspoon bicarbonate of soda
1 level teaspoon baking powder
$\frac{1}{2}$ teaspoon almond essence

Glaze
4 oz (100 g) sugar
$3\frac{1}{2}$ tablespoons fresh orange juice
4 tablespoons Grand Marnier
2 oz (50 g) sliced almonds (toasted) for garnish

Beat together until fluffy butter, sugar and egg yolks. Add sour cream and orange rind and blend thoroughly. Sift together flour, soda and baking powder and add to butter mixture. When smooth, fold in almond essence and egg whites and pour into a greased $3\frac{1}{2}$-pint ring mould. Bake for about 45 minutes, until the cake is risen and the top browned and firm. Remove to cooling rack and leave in tin. Make the orange glaze by stirring ingredients together over a medium heat until the sugar is dissolved, then pour over hot cake and decorate with almond slices. Allow to cool in tin completely before removing and storing.

Glazed lemon cake

This is a very pretty cake with a lot of rindy flavour to it. It can be made without the glaze and finished by dredging with sugar, but the glazed version is the nicest.

Yield: 1 loaf.
Keeps well for 2–3 days: after that the glaze tends to soften.
Oven: preheated to 350° (mark 4).

4 oz (100 g) soft butter
2 eggs
8 oz (200 g) sugar
finely grated rind of 2 lemons
6 oz (150 g) plain flour
1 level teaspoon baking powder
1 level teaspoon salt
4 fl oz (100 ml) milk
4 oz (100 g) walnuts, chopped (if using whole nuts, reserve 3
  or 4 halves to decorate top of cake)

Glaze
6 oz (150 g) sugar
2½ tablespoons fresh lemon juice

Beat together butter, eggs and sugar until fluffy. Stir in rind.
Sift together flour, baking powder and salt and add to butter
mixture, together with the milk, a little at a time. Stir in nuts
and pour into a greased 1 lb loaf tin. Bake for about an hour,
until cake is risen and the top firm and browned. Remove from
tin to a cooling rack. Make glaze by stirring ingredients together
over a medium heat until the sugar has melted, then pour over
cake, decorating top with walnut halves. Cool completely before
storing.

Fudge biscuit bake

This is a very rich cake which requires no baking. It can be
made in any flat-bottomed dish or round tin. Doubling the
recipe and using a soufflé dish works well.

Yield: 1 cake, 6- to 7-inch diameter.
Keeps well in a biscuit tin or covered in refrigerator.

3 level tablespoons golden syrup
10 oz (250 g) butter, preferably unsalted, melted
7 oz (175 g) plain unsweetened chocolate (Baker's preferably,
see p. 111), melted

6 oz (150 g) glacé cherries, roughly chopped
4 oz (100 g) sultanas, plumped in black coffee and drained
4 tablespoons rum
2 tablespoons hot water
6 oz (150 g) plain or digestive biscuits, broken into small
   pieces

Line tin with foil and grease lightly. Combine golden syrup,
chocolate, butter, cherries and sultanas. Combine rum and
water and add biscuits. When absorbed, add to all other ingredients and mix well. Pour into foil-lined tin, smooth to make
fit the shape of the tin and refrigerate until completely set.
Decant, peel off foil. Decorate with nuts if desired.

Alternative method: substitute 5 oz (125 g) unsweetened cocoa
powder and 11½ oz (287.5 g) butter for the chocolate and
butter quantities called for in basic recipe. You may want to
increase the golden syrup to suit your taste.

Variation: substitute chopped candied peel for the glacé
cherries, or a combination of peel and cherries. Adjust sweetness
of mixture by adding additional golden syrup if using peel alone.

Alcoholic drinks
and preserves

Giving alcoholic drinks and preserves

Timing is important when deciding what alcoholic preserves and drinks are candidates for gift-giving. As you will see in the following recipes, for the most part the element of time is required for the preserve or drink to attain the desired maturity and flavour. Hence, sadly, you can't decide to whip up a batch of sloe gin the day before you intend giving a bottle of it.

In the case of liqueurs, you will want to use clear glass bottles so the splendid reds and ambers of the fruit used are very much in evidence. Any bottle which can be securely corked or capped can be used. If you want to give a selection of liqueurs, try to use bottles of similar shapes and sizes, as these are easier to wrap attractively. When I am making liqueurs for gift-giving, I usually divide the liqueur between regular-sized clear wine bottles, and half bottles. Your local restaurant may well be thrilled at the prospect of your offering to take the empty bottles off the pile normally accumulating at the back of the kitchen. Always use new, clean corks, available from wine-making shops and most large chemists. Always wash the bottles with a bottle-brush, rinse thoroughly and allow to dry inside and out before use.

If you come across seconds in decanters or older glass at auctions, nothing could be nicer than giving your homemade liqueur in a re-usable decanter.

In the case of alcoholic preserves, follow the general advice on pp. 16 and 24.

Fruit-based liqueurs

Although the variety is infinite, the principle for making fruit-based liqueurs remains the same – the combination of fruit with sugar and a clear liquor (vodka, gin or eau-de-vie). Purists would say that the use of brandy, or indeed even gin, can mask the pure taste of the fruit used. Certainly only a clear liquor will give you the clarity of colour which is very much a part of the making of liqueurs. The fruit/sugar/liquor mixture is left to infuse for three months or more, before the liquid is strained through a double thickness of muslin to remove any cloudiness, and the resultant liquor decanted into bottles, tightly sealed and kept for six months to a year before giving or serving.

For the infusion process you will need large, clean glass jars with mouths sufficient to accommodate the fruit – ideally demi-johns, fitted with new, clean corks or tight-fitting lids. The most ready supplier is a wine-makers' shop. Once the infusion process has been accomplished, you will need several clear, sterilized bottles with tight-fitting screw-tops or new corks.

Proportions:
2 lb (800 g) fruit
2 pints (1 litre) liquor
1 lb (400 g) sugar

Note: Traditional recipes for liqueurs like Sloe Gin use a combination of white and brown sugars. You will get a heavier liqueur with a somewhat richer taste by using brown sugar; white sugar alone gives a truer fruit flavour and colour. I suggest that you experiment and suit your own taste.

Choose slightly under-ripe, unblemished fruit. Remove stalks, but not core if any. Wash and allow to dry completely. For fruit with durable skin (plums, damsons, sloes, apricots, peaches, pears, quinces, cherries, cranberries) prick all over with a sharp knife or skewer. For soft fruit (strawberries, raspberries, blackberries, mulberries) you will not need to prick. For citrus fruit, slice thinly and remove any pips.

Combine all ingredients in the demi-john(s), cork and put in a cool, dark place for three months. Remember to shake gently or turn the jar(s) several times a week to encourage the sugar to dissolve.

At the end of three months, strain the liqueur through muslin, several times if necessary, until the liqueur is completely clear. Pour into sterilized ½ litre bottles, seal tightly and keep in a cool, dark place. If you cannot resist the temptation to uncork them before six months is up, the liqueur will certainly be drinkable, but its smoothness and flavour does improve with age, so try to be patient for at least a year.

Suggested liqueurs:

Sloe Gin
Apricot Vodka (use half fresh apricots and half dried for best
  flavour)
Cranberry Vodka
Quince Eau-de-Vie
Prune Vodka (add half a lemon to the fruit)
Damson Vodka
Orange Gin

There is no reason why you can't experiment with a combination of fruits. Cranberry and Orange Vodka and Raspberry
and Peach Gin are particular favourites.

You may want to experiment with the fruit residue left
from the straining process. Not all the fruit residues are re-
cyclable, but the soft fruits puréed (they may need a bit more
sugar) as a sauce over ice cream and puddings can be a treat in
themselves.

Flavoured spirits

Many people who like gin and vodka are keen on flavoured, but
not sweet, spirits. The infusion process used in the previous
recipe works very well for non-sugared spirits, and the resultant
alcohol will have a pleasant scent and mild taste of whatever
herb (such as tarragon, thyme, or mint) you choose. The same
can be accomplished with the addition of cucumber, capsicum,
lemon rind or chillies. Infuse the mixture for about four months,
then strain through muslin to remove any sediment and re-
bottle.

Rumtof

This is a very inexact recipe, originating in the mists of time
from sources unknown. Whoever first conceived it must have
been a splendid souse, since even the breathing in of the fumes
is intoxicating. Basically, this is brandied soft fruit, made in
very large covered crocks so that you achieve not only a wonderful fruit concoction but a heady, fruity brandy as well.

The ideal vessel to make this in is a very large stone crock,
the bigger the better really. You need all this space as you will

be adding soft fruits to the mixture throughout the spring and summer as they become ripe.

The combination is fruit, with an equal amount of white sugar, covered by brandy. Layer after layer. Choose ripe, but not over-ripe fruit, free of blemish. Remove peel, stones, cores. Cut into bite-size pieces and put into crock. Add appropriate amount of sugar and just cover with brandy. The better the brandy, the better the result; but frankly, taking into account the price of brandy, I advise you to use your own judgement. The choice of fruit is yours, but you might want to avoid the heavily seeded berries, since the alcohol toughens the seeds.

Cover this wondrous mixture with the top of the crock or foil, but remember to stir several times a week, if not daily. Keep in a cool dark place. You keep adding fruits as they come into season, again adding an equal amount of sugar and making sure the mixture is just covered with brandy and the juice released by the sugar. When you stir the crock, breathe deeply and enjoy. The mixture will happily ferment all summer and it may well be difficult not to steal fruit from the crock.

By the middle of the autumn, when the last fruit in has been there for two to three months, the moment has come to enjoy. My suggestion is that you have a healthy go at the joys of the crock, but that you also store some of the mixture in preserving jars so as to make the joy last as long as possible. Pot as if the Rumtof was a pickle – i.e. decant into washed, dried and warmed preserving jars and seal. Depending upon the juiciness of the fruit, you may have a great deal of liquid. Use some of this with the fruit to be kept, and strain the rest to get rid of any cloudiness and sediment (several times if necessary) through double thicknesses of muslin. Decant into clean and dry bottles and cork. Serve as a liqueur, but only to those who deserve it.

Brandied fruit

The following recipe is adaptable to almost any soft fruit: peaches, pears, plums, apricots. Only make these fruits at the height of their availability, when they are at the peak of flavour and juiciness. The fruit should be under-ripe to just ripe and free of blemishes. I find that using smaller fruit makes the filling of jars easier, and peeling fruit is best accomplished by covering a few pieces at a time with boiling water: leave for a few minutes and the skins should slip off easily. You do not need to stone the fruit, as whole skinned fruit looks very nice, but you may prefer to slice the fruit in thick slices, which makes filling jars easier and means you can get more fruit to each jar. Use proper preserving jars for brandied fruit to eliminate any possibility of evaporation.

Keeps well, but should be used within the year. Store away from light to keep the colour perfect.

fruit: try 10 lb (4 kg) to start, peeled and cut up as desired
3 lb (1200 g) sugar
2 pints (1 litre) water
rind of 1 lemon, cut in thin strips
2 cinnamon sticks
2 level tablespoons whole cloves, heads removed, tied in
  muslin
4 pints (2 litres) brandy (you may need less)

Combine sugar and water in a big preserving pan and bring to the boil to make a syrup. Add spices and boil hard for 5 minutes. Remove from heat and remove spices. Add fruit and lemon rind and bring syrup back to the boil. Pack fruit densely into hot, sterilized preserving jars. Pour brandy half-way up the jars and top up to overflowing with syrup. Depress fruit to release trapped air and top up again with syrup. Seal.

Alcoholic prunes

Almost any dried fruits when plumped out with brandy, sherry, vermouth or the like taste marvellous. They can be eaten as sweetmeats, warmed gently in any remaining juice and served with cream, or used as the basis for fruit tarts. The jars shouldn't be packed too tightly as the fruit swells with the alcohol. Use proper preserving jars to eliminate all possibility of evaporation.

Yield: about 4 lb ($1\frac{1}{2}$ kg).
Keeps well up to 6 months in a cool, dark place.

3 lb (1200 g) pitted prunes of good quality
1 lb (400 g) light soft brown sugar
rind of 1 large lemon, cut into thin strips
1 pint (½ litre) brandy, sherry or vermouth (cheapest
    available)

Simmer prunes, covered with water, for about 5 minutes.
Remove from heat and allow to cool for about 10 minutes.
Strain liquid, retaining ¾ pint (375 ml). Pack prunes loosely in
preserving jars. Combine prune liquid, sugar and lemon rind
over a low heat until the sugar is completely dissolved. Boil
gently for 5 minutes. Remove from heat and pour evenly over
fruit, distributing between the jars. Fill the jars with liquor,
making sure the prunes are completely covered and the jars
filled to the top. Seal. Shake jars once a week to distribute
ingredients.

Variation: dried apricots, peaches or pears also make splendid
substitutes for prunes.

Mincemeat

There is nothing nicer than homemade mincemeat to give in
the holiday season. You should use proper preserving jars for
this.

Yield: 6–8 lb (about 3 kg).
Keeps very well. It can and should be made at least a month
before using to allow the flavours to mature.

1 lb (400 g) currants
1 lb (400 g) seedless white raisins or sultanas
1 lb (400 g) seedless raisins
1 lb (400 g) chopped mixed peel
1 lb (400 g) cooking apples, peeled, cored and roughly
    chopped
4 oz (100 g) sweet almonds, blanched
2 oz (50 g) bitter almonds, blanched
juice and coarsely grated rind of 1 large lemon
juice and coarsely grated rind of 1 large orange
2 carrots, coarsely grated

1 lb (400 g) dark soft brown sugar
8 oz (200 g) shredded suet
1 level teaspoon ground nutmeg
1 level teaspoon ground cinnamon
1 level teaspoon ground cloves
1 level teaspoon ground allspice
brandy, rum or whisky to moisten

Combine all ingredients in a large bowl or preserving pan and mix thoroughly. The mixture should be moist, not sodden, so add liquor accordingly. Cover with a tea-towel and leave in a cool (important) dark place for 2 days. Stir each day and add more liquor if the mixture seems dry or very stiff. Pack into hot, sterilized preserving jars, screw down lids, and place jars in a roasting pan with water to mid-jar and leave in a 250° (mark ½) oven for 1½ hours. Check lids are tight before storing.

Index

Index